Varieties of Postmodern Theology

SUNY SERIES IN
CONSTRUCTIVE POSTMODERN THOUGHT
DAVID RAY GRIFFIN, EDITOR

David Ray Griffin, editor, *The Reenchantment of Science: Postmodern Proposals*

David Ray Griffin, editor, *Spirituality and Society: Postmodern Visions*

David Ray Griffin, *God and Religion in the Postmodern World: Essays in Postmodern Theology*

David Ray Griffin, William A. Beardslee, and Joe Holland, *Varieties of Postmodern Theology*

VARIETIES

—————— OF ——————

POSTMODERN
THEOLOGY

BT
28
.G754
1989

DAVID RAY GRIFFIN
WILLIAM A. BEARDSLEE
JOE HOLLAND

STATE UNIVERSITY OF NEW YORK PRESS

Published by
State University of New York Press, Albany
© *1989 State University of New York*

Printed in the United States of America

*For information, address State University of New York
Press, State University Plaza, Albany, N.Y., 12246*

Library of Congress Cataloging-in-Publication Data

Griffin, David Ray, 1939-
*Varieties of postmodern theology / David Ray Griffin, William A.
Beardslee, Joe Holland.*
p.   cm. — *(SUNY series in constructive postmodern thought)*
Includes index.
ISBN 0-7914-0050-6.   ISBN 0-7914-0051-4 (pbk.)
*1. Theology, Doctrinal—History—20th century.   2. Postmodernism.
I. Beardslee, William A.   II. Holland, Joe.   III. Title.   IV. Title:
Title: Postmodern theology.   V. Series.*
BT28.G754 1989   88-13923
230'.09'04—dc 19   CIP

10 9 8 7 6 5 4 3 2 1

for John B. Cobb, Jr.,
sine qua non

CONTENTS

ACKNOWLEDGMENTS

An earlier version of Joe Holland's first essay was published, under the title "The Post-Modern Paradigm Implicit in the Church's Shift to the Left," in *Faith that Transforms: Essays in Honor of Gregory Baum,* ed. Mary Jo Leddy, N.D.S., and Mary Ann Hinsdale, I.H.M. (New York/Mahwah, N.J.: Paulist Press, 1987), and is republished here in revised form with permission of the editors and the publisher. This essay had been earlier distributed in manuscript form by the Center of Concern, 3700 13th Street, N.E., Washington, D.C. 20017, and is republished with its permission as well. The latter half of Holland's second essay is a revision of "John Paul II on the Laity in Society: The Spiritual Transformation of Modern Culture," which was published in *Social Thought,* Spring/Summer 1987, and is reprinted in revised form with permission. The essays by Beardslee and Griffin on Cornel West's theology were originally prepared for a dialogue between West and several process theologians arranged by the Center for Process Studies in Claremont, March 9–10, 1986. The present versions have benefitted from the extended conversation with West. Griffin's essay on Mark Taylor has benefitted from a response by Taylor to an earlier draft.

We are grateful to the School of Theology at Claremont and the Claremont University Center and Graduate School for support of the Center for Process Studies, to the members who support the Center for a Postmodern World, to Geneva Villegas for cheerful and fast typing, to William Eastman of SUNY Press for being enthusiastic about this series in general and this volume in particular, and to Elizabeth Moore for shepherding this volume through the publication process.

The technical artwork for the figures was done by Mary K. Siegel of Santa Barbara.

INTRODUCTION TO SUNY SERIES IN CONSTRUCTIVE POSTMODERN THOUGHT

The rapid spread of the term *postmodern* in recent years witnesses to a growing dissatisfaction with modernity and to an increasing sense that the modern age not only had a beginning but can have an end as well. Whereas the word *modern* was almost always used until quite recently as a word of praise and as a synonym for *contemporary*, a growing sense is now evidenced that we can and should leave modernity behind—in fact, that we *must* if we are to avoid destroying ourselves and most of the life on our planet.

Modernity, rather than being regarded as the norm for human society toward which all history has been aiming and into which all societies should be ushered—forcibly if necessary—is instead increasingly seen as an aberration. A new respect for the wisdom of traditional societies is growing as we realize that they have endured for thousands of years and that, by contrast, the existence of modern society for even another century seems doubtful. Likewise, *modernism* as a worldview is less and less seen as The Final Truth, in comparison with which all divergent worldviews are automatically regarded as "superstitious." The modern worldview is increasingly relativized to the status of one among many, useful for some purposes, inadequate for others.

Although there have been antimodern movements before, beginning perhaps near the outset of the nineteenth century with the Romanticists and the Luddites, the rapidity with which the term *postmodern* has become widespread in our time suggests that the antimodern sentiment is more extensive and intense than before, and also that it includes the sense that modernity can be successfully overcome only by going beyond it, not by

xi

attempting to return to a premodern form of existence. Insofar as a common element is found in the various ways in which the term is used, *postmodernism* refers to a diffuse sentiment rather than to any common set of doctrines—the sentiment that humanity can and must go beyond the modern.

Beyond connoting this sentiment, the term *postmodern* is used in a confusing variety of ways, some of them contradictory to others. In artistic and literary circles, for example, postmodernism shares in this general sentiment but also involves a specific reaction against "modernism" in the narrow sense of a movement in artistic-literary circles in the late nineteenth and early twentieth centuries. Postmodern architecture is very different from postmodern literary criticism. In some circles, the term *postmodern* is used in reference to that potpourri of ideas and systems sometimes called *new age metaphysics,* although many of these ideas and systems are more premodern than postmodern. Even in philosophical and theological circles, the term *postmodern* refers to two quite different positions, one of which is reflected in this series. Each position seeks to transcend both *modernism* in the sense of the worldview that has developed out of the seventeenth century Galilean-Cartesian-Baconian-Newtonian science, and *modernity* in the sense of the world order that both conditioned and was conditioned by this worldview. But the two positions seek to transcend the modern in different ways.

Closely related to literary-artistic postmodernism is a philosophical postmodernism inspired variously by pragmatism, physicalism, Ludwig Wittgenstein, Martin Heidegger, and Jacques Derrida and other recent French thinkers. By the use of terms that arise out of particular segments of this movement, it can be called *deconstructive* or *eliminative postmodernism.* It overcomes the modern worldview through an anti-worldview: it deconstructs or eliminates the ingredients necessary for a worldview, such as God, self, purpose, meaning, a real world, and truth as correspondence. While motivated in some cases by the ethical concern to forestall totalitarian systems, this type of postmodern thought issues in relativism, even nihilism. It could also be called *ultramodernism,* in that its eliminations result from carrying modern premises to their logical conclusions.

The postmodernism of this series can, by contrast, be called *constructive* or *revisionary.* It seeks to overcome the modern worldview not by eliminating the possibility of worldviews as such, but by constructing a postmodern worldview through a revision of modern premises and traditional concepts. This constructive or revisionary postmodernism involves a new unity of scientific, ethical, aesthetic, and religious intuitions. It rejects not science as such but only that scientism in which the data of the modern natural sciences are alone allowed to contribute to the construction of our worldview.

The constructive activity of this type of postmodern thought is not limited to a revised worldview; it is equally concerned with a postmodern world that will support and be supported by the new worldview. A postmodern world will involve postmodern persons, with a postmodern spirituality, on the one hand, and a postmodern society, ultimately a postmodern global order, on the other. Going beyond the modern world will involve transcending its individualism, anthropocentrism, patriarchy, mechanization, economism, consumerism, nationalism, and militarism. Constructive postmodern thought provides support for the ecology, peace, feminist, and other emancipatory movements of our time, while stressing that the inclusive emancipation must be from modernity itself. The term *postmodern*, however, by contrast with *premodern*, emphasizes that the modern world has produced unparalleled advances that must not be lost in a general revulsion against its negative features.

From the point of view of deconstructive postmodernists, this constructive postmodernism is still hopelessly wedded to outdated concepts, because it wishes to salvage a positive meaning not only for the notions of the human self, historical meaning, and truth as correspondence, which were central to modernity, but also for premodern notions of a divine reality, cosmic meaning, and an enchanted nature. From the point of view of its advocates, however, this revisionary postmodernism is not only more adequate to our experience but also more genuinely postmodern. It does not simply carry the premises of modernity through to their logical conclusions, but criticizes and revises those premises. Through its return to organicism and its acceptance of nonsensory perception, it opens itself to the recovery of truths and values from various forms of premodern thought and practice that had been dogmatically rejected by modernity. This constructive, revisionary postmodernism involves a creative synthesis of modern and premodern truths and values.

This series does not seek to create a movement so much as to help shape and support an already existing movement convinced that modernity can and must be transcended. But those antimodern movements which arose in the past failed to deflect or even retard the onslaught of modernity. What reasons can we have to expect the current movement to be more successful? First, the previous antimodern movements were primarily calls to return to a premodern form of life and thought rather than calls to advance, and the human spirit does not rally to calls to turn back. Second, the previous antimodern movements either rejected modern science, reduced it to a description of mere appearances, or assumed its adequacy in principle; therefore, they could base their calls only on the negative social and spiritual effects of modernity. The current movement draws on natural science itself as a witness against the adequacy of the modern worldview. In the third place, the present movement has even more evidence than did previous movements of the ways in which modernity and its worldview *are* socially and spiritually destructive. The fourth and probably most decisive difference is that the present movement is based on the awareness that *the continuation of modernity threatens the very survival of life on our planet.*

This awareness, combined with the growing knowledge of the interdependence of the modern worldview and the militarism, nuclearism, and ecological devastation of the modern world, is providing an unprecedented impetus for people to see the evidence for a postmodern worldview and to envisage postmodern ways of relating to each other, the rest of nature, and the cosmos as a whole. For these reasons, the failure of the previous antimodern movements says little about the possible success of the current movement.

Advocates of this movement do not hold the naively utopian belief that the success of this movement would bring about a global society of universal and lasting peace, harmony, and happiness, in which all spiritual problems, social conflicts, ecological destruction, and hard choices would vanish. There is, after all, surely a deep truth in the testimony of the world's religions to the presence of a transcultural proclivity to evil deep within the human heart, which no new paradigm, combined with a new economic order, new child-rearing practices, or any other social arrangements, will suddenly eliminate. Furthermore, it has correctly been said that "life is robbery": a strong element of competition is inherent within finite existence, which no social-political-economic-ecological order can overcome. These two truths, especially when contemplated together, should caution us against unrealistic hopes.

However, no such appeal to "universal constants" should reconcile us to the present order, as if this order were thereby uniquely legitimated. The human proclivity to evil in general, and to conflictual competition and ecological destruction in particular, can be greatly exacerbated or greatly mitigated by a world order and its worldview. Modernity exacerbates it about as much as imaginable. We can therefore envision, without being naively utopian, a far better world order, with a far less dangerous trajectory, than the one we now have.

This series, making no pretense of neutrality, is dedicated to the success of this movement toward a postmodern world.

David Ray Griffin
Series Editor

1

INTRODUCTION: VARIETIES OF POSTMODERN THEOLOGY

David Ray Griffin

This book deals with eight types of postmodern theology—or, one could equally say, four basic types, with each type having two versions. To call all of them types of *postmodern* theology is to imply that they all have something in common. To speak of *varieties* is to indicate that significant differences exist among them. Indeed, the phrase *postmodern theology* is suddenly being used for a very diverse set of programs. The differences among them are probably more obvious than their similarities.

The varieties of postmodern theology do have some features in common. A not insignificant fact is that they all use the term *postmodern*. The various theologians thereby register their conviction that that noble and flawed enterprise called *modern theology* has run its course. Exactly how "modern theology" should be characterized is a question that elicits different answers. But even here there are commonalities. Modern theology, it can be agreed, sought to articulate the essence of the biblical faith in a context in which the general cultural consciousness was assumed to be shaped by the modern worldview, and in which a rational, objective approach to reality, through the natural and social sciences, was assumed to support the modern worldview. The varieties of modern theology represented different strategies for "doing theology" within that context, which at first glance seemed to make theology impossible. The major divide is between early and late modern theologies. Early modern theology, represented most clearly by the deists of the eighteenth century, sought to accommodate theology to the modern worldview by reducing theology's content, often by "demythologizing" it. It was hoped by many that this procedure would produce a universal theology representing the essence of all the religions. This universal theology would provide a religious but nonsectarian basis for public policy. The attempt to work out this strategy led many to the conclusion, however, that it so diluted the content of biblical faith that it left the religious community with an inadequate basis for identity and the individual with an inadequate basis for facing the perils of modern existence. Early modern theology's twin goals of universality and integrity seemed incompatible. This perception led to late modern theology's decision to retain religious identity and integrity through a return to particularity. Late modern theology gave up its claim to universality and thereby its claim to provide a basis for public policy in an increasingly pluralistic society.

From that characteristic of late modern theology followed two others, both of which were aspects of its nonpublic nature. On the one hand, late modern theology appealed to criteria of validation other than the public criteria used in science and science-based philosophy, that is, self-consistency and adequacy to generally accessible facts. Whether late modern theologians spoke of truth as subjectivity, contrasted the perspective (or "language game") of objective science with that of religion, or appealed to a revelation to a particular community which allowed them to speak "from faith to faith," they conceded the arena of public discourse to the modern worldview. In so doing, these theologians excused themselves from the need to meet the demands of public verification. On the other hand, late modern theology sought to articulate biblical faith in a context in which people's faith, religion, or piety was generally assumed to be a private matter, without relevance to public policy. These two nonpublic features of late modern theology were related: insofar as the implications of a community's religious faith remained private, the criteria for evaluating its assertions could also be private.

Given this characterization, it is obvious that not all theologies during the modern period were equally modern. For example, many philosophical theologies prior to the rise of the term *postmodern* were postmodern with regard to using only public criteria of validation. The could do this without evacuating biblical faith of its content because they challenged some of the basic presuppositions of the modern worldview. And "social gospel" theologies sought to be relevant to public policy. Reinhold Niebuhr, who both worked largely within a Whiteheadian-Hartshornean philosophical framework and retained most of the emphases of the social gospel, was about half modern and half postmodern.

In speaking of *postmodern* theology, then, the various theologies using this self-designation share both a common view of the nature of modern theology and a common conviction that its era is over.

Beyond these formal agreements, great variety is to be found among the postmodern theologies. The four basic types discussed in this volume can be called (1) constructive (or revisionary), (2) deconstructive (or eliminative), (3) liberationist, and (4) restorationist (or conservative). Constructive or revisionary postmodern theology is the specifically theological dimension of the constructive postmodern thought to which this series is devoted and which is discussed in the introduction to the series, above. One version of this type is represented in the essays by William Beardslee and me. Those of its general features that are especially stressed by me are discussed in the introduction to my companion volume, *God and Religion in the Postmodern World*. A second version of constructive or revisionary postmodern theology is exemplified by Joe Holland. Whereas Beardslee and I are Protestants and stand in the tradition of Whiteheadian process theology, Holland is a Roman Catholic whose perspective is shaped more by Thomas Berry's ecologized Teilhardianism, Matthew Fox's creation-centered spirituality, and the transformed Heideggerianism of Gibson Winter's *Liberating Creation*.

This type of postmodern theology rejects all the characteristics of late modern theology mentioned above. While it recognizes that Western culture is still overwhelmingly shaped by the modern worldview, it believes that this situation is rapidly changing. The change is coming about in part, it holds, because the objective (rational-empirical) approach to reality no longer supports the modern worldview, but is pointing instead toward a postmodern worldview. And it believes that theology must in our time become public in both senses: it must make its case in terms of the criteria of self-consistency and adequacy to generally accessible facts of experience, and it must be directly relevant to matters of public policy.

Deconstructive or eliminative postmodern thought is also discussed in the general introduction to the series. The term *deconstruction* properly belongs, of course, to the French-based movement in which Jacques Derrida is the most prominent figure, and behind which stands Heidegger's deconstruction of Western metaphysics. This type of postmodern thought as represented by Jean-François Lyotard is discussed in Beardslee's first essay and, as represented by Mark C. Taylor, in my first essay. The term *eliminative* comes from a position that emerged in English-language philosophy sometimes called *eliminative materialism,* of which Richard Rorty has been a central advocate. This version of postmodern philosophy is also discussed in the critiques of Cornel West's theology. The positions of Taylor and West represent two very different ways to relate theology to this type of postmodern philosophy.

This type of postmodern philosophy believes that an objective approach to the facts of experience proves, paradoxically, that an objective approach is not possible, and that this realization undermines the modern worldview along with every other worldview. It believes that we are moving into a postmodern age in which this relativistic outlook will increasingly undermine the modern worldview.

The two forms of theology based on this type of postmodern philosophy have quite different ways of going public in relation to it. Taylor takes the deconstructive postmodern outlook as definitive of the context for theology, which must thereby become "a/theology." No private revelation or alternative perspective can circumvent the negative conclusions of the deconstructive analysis. Although positive motives generally lie behind this postmodern a/theology, its direct relevance to public policy is primarily negative: it is content for the most part simply to undermine the social structures that have been based on modern assumptions. The theology of Cornel West, by contrast, provides positive support for movements for human liberation. It has done this, however, by apparently retaining one of the features of late modern (and premodern) theology mentioned above: an appeal to a particular (the Christian) community's faith which is not evaluated in terms of the criteria of self-consistency and adequacy to generally available facts of experience. Unlike constructive postmodern theologians, West does not point to a postmodern worldview; unlike Taylor, he does not limit the theologian's affirmations to those consistent with deconstructive analysis. West's position involves an interesting combination of liberationist faith and eliminative postmodern philosophy.

Other examples of deconstructive postmodern theology are extant. They include Carl A. Raschke, *The Alchemy of the Word: Language and the End of Theology* (Missoula, Mont: Scholars Press, 1979), Jeffrey Stout, *The Flight from Authority: Religion, Morality, and the Quest for Autonomy* (Notre Dame, Ind.: University of Notre Dame Press, 1981, which is invaluable for its elucidation of the history of foundationalism and the reaction thereto, and Charles Winquist, *Epiphanies of Darkness: Deconstruction in Theology* (Philadelphia: Fortress Press, 1986). Each has its distinctive emphases. But the main presuppositions and contentions of this movement are, I believe, discussed in the treatments of Lyotard, Taylor, and West herein.

The third type of postmodern theology is liberationist. While Cornel West provides one version of liberationist postmodern theology, Harvey Cox provides a second. Unlike the other types of postmodern theologians, Cox does not raise the issue of whether an objective analysis of the facts of experience undermines the modern worldview. But he does argue that theologians should not be constrained by the cultural mind-set that has been shaped by this worldview. The primary concern of a postmodern theology, in Cox's view, is to be liberationist, and for this purpose it can build most effectively upon the premodern piety of the religious communities. While Cox's theology is clearly postmodern in seeking to overcome the privatization of faith, it retains late modern theology's rejection of the need for theology to be self-consistent and adequate to the various facts of experience. On this point, it should be added, my characterization of modern theology and Cox's diverge: he believes that this concern with adequacy and especially consistency has been an obsession in modern theology which a properly postmodern theology will overcome. He thereby regards a feature of early modern theology as characteristic of modern theology as a whole. Liberationist postmodern theology, I should add, is also discussed in Joe Holland's first essay.

The fourth type of postmodern theology can be called restorationist or conservative. This form of postmodern theology has thus far appeared mostly in Roman Catholic theologians, although the Lutheran Richard John Neuhaus manifests some affinity with it in *The Catholic Moment: The Paradox of the Church in the Postmodern World* (San Francisco: Harper & Row, 1987). We have only one essay on conservative postmodern theology, this being Joe Holland's essay on the cultural theology of Pope John Paul II. To maintain symmetry with our treatment of other types of postmodern theology, in which we present two versions of each type, I here summarize briefly another version of this type, that provided by George William Rutler in *Beyond Modernity: Reflections of a Post-Modern Catholic* (San Francisco: Ignatius Press, 1987). I indicate how this version of restorationist postmodern theology compares with the constructive postmodern theology embodied in this volume.

Rutler's restorationist postmodernism contains much that resonates with the opinions of constructive postmodern theologians. Much of this agreement involves the features of modernity that are rejected. Rutler rejects modernism's relativism, subjectivism, reductionism, scientism, and sensate empiricism (22-24, 30, 35, 98, 193), together with its assumption that it is the final standard of all truth and value (11, 27). He wants to overcome modernity's utilitarianism, consumerism, individualism, loneliness, alienation, dependence on independence, and loss of memory (25, 63, 35-37, 46, 57, 77, 97-98). Rutler rejects both the totalitarianism in socialist countries and the sensuality and moral indifference in capitalist countries to which these features of modernism and modernity lead (28). Some commonality is also found with regard to the kind of postmodern world envisioned. Much of this commonality is constituted by the obvious opposites of the rejected features of modernity just mentioned. Besides these features, Rutler looks forward to a new union of religion and politics, and of theology and science, and thereby to a transformation of the pluriversity back into a university (13, 29-31, 85).

The differences from the postmodern theology represented in this book and series, however, are at least as significant as the commonalities. Rutler's so-called *post*modernism differs little from earlier forms of Roman Catholic *anti*modernism. Indeed, his heroes include Cardinal Newman as well as Cardinal Ratzinger (33, 197, 199, 200). Rutler does deny that he is simply advocating archaism or revivalism (34); but, besides saying that "anything valuable of post-modern life will be that which was valuable in pre-modern life" (29), he seems to recommend a simple return to medieval theology, especially that of Thomas Aquinas. No creative synthesis of medieval with modern insights seems to be in view. There is no sign, for example, that anthropocentric and androcentric assumptions are to be modified through the impact of the ecological and feminist movements: Rutler speaks of "Christian humanism," and uses "man" for human beings (37 and *passim*). Nor is Christian faith to be enlarged by insights from other religious traditions. Rutler's postmodern Christianity will not even be one that unites Protestants and Catholics: all his remarks about Protestantism are critical, and he even repeats the characterization of Luther as the "elemental barbarian" (36, 41, 97). Pluralism will be overcome, not celebrated, in Rutler's postmodern world. The new unity of religion and politics is to be a reunion of Christianity and politics—more particularly, *Catholicism* and politics. Rutler's vision, in fact, is the restoration of the unity of the Catholic worldview and world order that was destroyed through Protestantism and the Enlightenment (65–66, 96, 98). Overcoming modernism will mean a return to revealed, immutable doctrines (33, 34, 193) and the recognition of papal infallibility (43, 51, 194, 202). Rutler's solution to our problems is perhaps best summed up in the following statement: "modern man fell apart as he lost the moral and spiritual unity of his culture. Only loyalty to the chair of Peter, the seat of unity, can secure freedom of life and humaneness of humanity. . . . [F]reedom requires conformity to the structure of Christ's Body as it is made visible in the hierarchical constitution of the Church" (220, 222). This type of postmodern theology, at least in this version, therefore does not share the conviction that a public theology must employ public criteria of validity.

In his account of the theology of John Paul II, Joe Holland shows it to be a significantly different version of restorationist or conservative postmodern theology, one that may be open to supplementation by the constructive postmodernism embodied in this series.

While four types of postmodern theology—constructive, deconstructive, liberationist, and restorationist—are discussed herein, they are by no means presented neutrally. As indicated, this book is part of a series in which constructive postmodern thought is advocated, and all the essays are written from this perspective. Beardslee, Holland, and I claim that the valid points made by the other types of postmodern theology can be expressed, and can be expressed better because in a more balanced way, within a constructive or revisionary postmodern theology. It is possible that the proponents of the other types of postmodern theology will immediately and unanimously agree. Barring that improbable possibility, however, I hope this book will contribute to vigorous public debate about the nature and purpose of theology in our time. Even some defenders of modern theology may want to join in.

I take special pride in being able to use this series to present to a new audience the writings of two of the most profound postmodern thinkers,

William Beardslee and Joe Holland, whose writings have previously earned them great respect but within quite limited circles. (Readers of the second volume of this series, *Spirituality and Society: Postmodern Visions*, will have encountered Holland before.) Beardslee has long been a respected figure within biblical studies and process theology, and has been the recognized leader in relating these two fields of interest. Holland's ideas have thus far been known primarily within Roman Catholic circles devoted to revitalizing the laity. The essays by the two of them in this volume reveal something of the inclusive scope as well as the subtlety of their thought. Because of Beardslee's gifts as a historian and exegete, his essays, with their attention to the authors' intentions within their historical contexts, provide a nice balance to my more abstract, philosophical treatments. Another form of balance and richness is provided by Holland, who approaches the contrast between premodern, modern, and postmodern with a sociologist's sensitivities. It would be too little to say that I have been "greatly informed" by the writings of Beardslee and Holland; their writings have had something of the force of revelation for me. I trust that this will be true for others.

The dedication of the volume to John Cobb is appropriate not only because without him it would not exist, but also because he first used the term *postmodern* (in a 1964 essay) for the type of philosophical theology reflected herein.

2

THE POSTMODERN
PARADIGM AND
CONTEMPORARY
CATHOLICISM

Joe Holland

Recently many have noted that the Catholic Church is undergoing a dramatic transformation. In this essay, I unfold the hypothesis that this transformation, while destabilizing the Church's working alliance with liberalism or capitalism during the twentieth century, implicitly contains *a postliberal, post-Marxist, and even a postmodern social and religious paradigm.* I propose further that it contains implicitly the seeds of a new ecumenical Christian theology.

It has been often argued that this Catholic transformation represents a Catholic surrender to Marxism or to the secular humanism of modern liberalism. [1] But I am proposing that, while the transformation has occurred within the context of a new Catholic encounter with both modern Marxism and modern liberalism, the actual Catholic praxis (if not the articulated theory) nevertheless increasingly carries an implicitly postmodern paradigm.

The Catholic transformation remains open to liberalism and to Marxism, but it begins to transform both from within. It does this by profoundly shifting the foundational vision.

In proposing this hypothesis, I first sketch the end of the cultural period called the modern world. Then, I sequentially review the classical Catholic paradigm, the initial modern liberal paradigm, and the Marxian radicalization of the modern liberal paradigm.[2] Next, I sketch the newly emerging postmodern paradigm, proposed as implicit in aspects of contemporary Catholic practice. Finally, I conclude with some theological observations about ecumenical possibilities within the postmodern paradigm.

There is space in this essay to do no more than to unfold the hypothesis by contrasting what I propose as the emerging postmodern paradigm with an interpretation of prior modern and classical paradigms. I will therefore not argue for the truth of this hypothesis nor chronicle its development in historical events. The hypothesis functions here as an intuitive proposal, what Paul Ricoeur would call a hermeneutical "guess" to guide further work.[3]

I. THE END OF THE MODERN WORLD

The modern world as a coherent period of social history began seminally with the sixteenth century, matured after the eighteenth century, and now in the late twentieth century is coming to an end.

Prior to the sixteenth century, a premodern consciousness still dominated the West. This meant a fatalistic acceptance of nature and history, with all their limits and tragedies, as reflecting God's immutable ordering of the world. Individual giants such as empire builders obviously defied fate to change history, but even they saw themselves as the carriers of fate and represented oppressive fate to those whom they controlled. There have been many names for the various forms of this premodern period in the life of the West, such as *traditional society, classical society,* and *feudalism.*

By contrast, the modern spirit promised to liberate humanity from fate. It promised to break the religiously legitimated constraints of classical Catholic tradition and its authoritarian institutions. It promised a new vision, centered in secular science seeking freedom and progress for all the world.

Renaissance humanism was midwife to this new cultural worldview and the Protestant Reformation gave it a religious ground. But its full birth came forth in the Enlightenment. The Enlightenment promised to use the light of reason to shatter all residues of superstition and ignorance. It became the intellectual foundation for the modern world.[4]

The modern world unleashed humanity's productive powers of control over nature and history. Compared to the modern scientific world, all prior history marked but the infancy or even prehistory of humanity. For thousands of years, human civilization had wandered in a prescientific consciousness, immersed in biological, historical, and above all religious fate. Yet, in a few hundred years, the modern world changed everything.

The modern world ushered in a trajectory of ever-expanding progress, whereby the wonders of one generation became but the stepping-off point for the next. Secret mathematical theories of tiny elites of priests and philosophers in ages past became the simple working tools of millions of young school children. The modern world freed technology, politics, economics, and culture from nearly every restraint. So powerful was this modern vision that today it has become the only way many of us can conceive reality.

In the late twentieth century, however, the modern vision grows culturally weary. The reason? Its vision of human freedom and progress is backfiring.

The result of the modern world is increasingly a new, more powerful, and destructive technological fate. The modern world has begun to build a scientific death trap for humanity and nature. More powerful than premodern fate, this modern version threatens to destroy humanity and the earth. Even short of total destruction, late modern fate has already unleashed great forces of interim destruction.

Only in the twentieth century did the destructive side of the modern world become clear. Only in this generation did consciousness of it spread widely across our culture.

The first major expression was World War I, a war of terrible technological ferocity eroding the distinction between soldier and civilian. It was justified as a final act, a war to end all war. Soon after came World War II, infinitely more destructive with the protracted saturation bombing of Dresden and the instantaneous atomic bombings of Hiroshima and Nagasaki. Contemplating this fate, Pope Pius XII wrote: "There will be no song of victory, only the inconsolable weeping of humanity, which in desolation will gaze upon the catastrophe brought on by its own folly."

Two other modern abominations arose in the twentieth century. The first was the rise of scientific totalitarian states from both capitalism and socialism. The second was the attempted scientific extermination of European Jewry and of millions of other reputed enemies of the Nazi State.

Later, other themes of destruction would come before the late modern consciousness. The most powerful recently has been awareness of the slow poisoning of the natural ecology of the planet. A still more subtle one has been what might be called the poisoning of humanity's social ecology: the steady erosion of the delicate fabric of family, neighborhood, and community, and their underlying moral values. Perhaps the overriding theme is fear of nuclear destruction.

Meanwhile, in the midst of the greatest technological productivity of all human history, the poor are systematically excluded, in even larger numbers than before, to a structural underclass. Beneath all this grows an ever deepening secularization, shutting out from public life the awe and power of the religious Mystery.

Thus, we see the negative climax of the modern scientific promise of freedom and progress: ever more destructive wars, threats of nuclear annihilation, genocide, totalitarianism, ecological poisoning, erosion of community, marginalization of the poor, and public suppression of religious Mystery.[5] What emerged in the eighteenth century as a bold dream converts itself dialectically in the late twentieth century into a frightening nightmare. This is the cultural end of the modern world.[6]

Currently, two modern scientific ideologies do battle with each other over who shall triumph in this crisis-ridden modern culture. But by so doing they deepen their mutual path of violence across nature and history. These two ideologies are liberalism and Marxism, or scientific industrial capitalism and scientific industrial socialism, typified by the United States and the Soviet Union. Actually, the two are symbiotic expressions of the same dialectical thrust of the Enlightenment. Both are headed on a path of converging destruction.

Both liberalism and Marxism are ideologies of modern secular freedom and progress. They share common roots in the Enlightenment vision. Marxism has not provided a radical alternative to liberalism, only a radicalization of it. And liberalism, rather than providing an alternative to the totalitarian expression of Marxism in Soviet orthodox communism, is now generating a parallel and convergent crisis. The modern cultural crisis is thus not of one or the other modern ideology, but of modernity itself.

At the foundation of both modern ideologies is the common root metaphor of the machine, as the cultural image of nature and humanity.[7] It is a machine, however, that is increasingly turning against humanity and nature. I elaborate on this mechanistic root metaphor in section III. First, however, I review how the premodern, classical Catholic worldview perceived reality.

II. THE CLASSICAL PARADIGM:
HIERARCHICAL ORGANICISM

Ideologies, or more broadly worldviews, can be examined in terms of their interpretation of the following elements: (1) time, (2) space, (3) the holy, (4) governance, and (5) root metaphor. I propose the following interpretation of the classical worldview.

1. *Time:* The future was seen as a continuation of the past. History was seen as a broad repetitive cycle of biological birth and decay, but with a nonhistorical cosmic core of eternal truth providing the transcendent "soul" of the civilization, protected by abiding, fortress-like institutions. This combination of fortress and

transcendence also provided the foundation for the West's symbiosis of uprooted metaphysics and political imperialism.

2. *Space:* Hierarchical order was the basic structure, with cycles of material regeneration and degeneration marking the lowest regions and sexless transcendent spirituality marking the highest ones.

Figure A—The Classical Catholic Vision

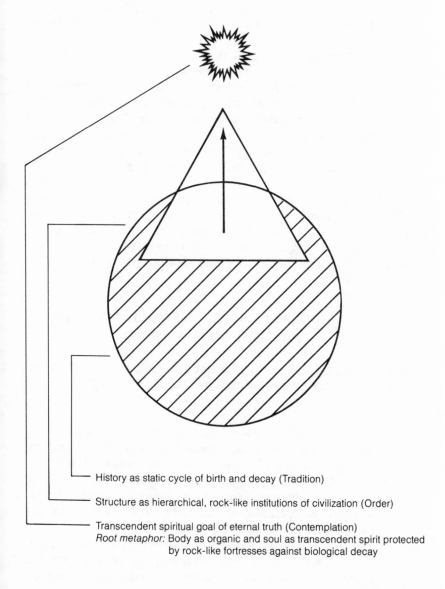

History as static cycle of birth and decay (Tradition)

Structure as hierarchical, rock-like institutions of civilization (Order)

Transcendent spiritual goal of eternal truth (Contemplation)
Root metaphor: Body as organic and soul as transcendent spirit protected
by rock-like fortresses against biological decay

Hierarchy was the key structural principle, in which the lower existed for the higher.

3. *The Holy:* In this nonhistorical, hierarchical view, all reality emanated from and returned to the divine source as in a great chain of being. All reality was thus religious, although biological life was remote from the divine. The holy apex was the transcendent control point, with its worship fortified in heavy institutions.

4. *Governance:* Rule was its form of governance. It was hierarchically exercised from the top down, in order to protect the tradition, preserve the order, and worship the holy. Rule had a religious character.

5. *Root Metaphor:* Externally, the basic metaphor of imagination was the hierarchically interpreted biological body. Nature and society were modeled on Aristotelian biology. But the body was ordered to higher spiritual transcendence, namely the "soul" of the civilization encased in rock-like institutions immune from the biological cycle of birth and decay, and witnessed to by the exclusion of sexuality from the sanctuary.[8] The full root metaphor encompassed a dualism of body and soul, organicity and hierarchy.

The premodern or classical Catholic vision was, therefore, one of static tradition, fixed order, hierarchical rule, unchanging institutions, and transcendent sacralism, all founded on a mixed metaphor combining the biological with the hierarchical, witnessed to by a rock-like fortress. Body, soul, and rock all went together. This was the vision of Christian Civilization or Christendom.[9]

III. THE MODERN CHALLENGE FROM LIBERALISM: PHYSICAL MECHANISM

The first ideological challenge to this classical or premodern Catholic worldview came from the modern ideology of liberalism.[10] The pattern of its worldview is as follows:

1. *Time:* Liberalism unleashed the future in an evolutionary trajectory (progress) by rejecting the past. This was a dualistic temporal axis of evolutionary modernization versus traditional stasis.

2. *Space:* Liberalism shattered the former order of the hierarchical whole by maximizing the autonomy of the parts (freedom) in the whirling competition of economics (capitalism), politics (democracy), and culture (free thought).

3. *The Holy:* Liberalism produced a progressive privatization and marginalization of religious energies in order to expand the autonomy of the secular, advanced by science and technology.

Autonomous science and technology became the religion of the public realm, while individualistic pietism became the religion of the private realm. Both the biological cycle and the contemplative transcendence of the classical pattern were dissolved into the linear drive of the machine for production (activism), compensated by private refuge in home and religion.

Figure B—The Modern Liberal Vision

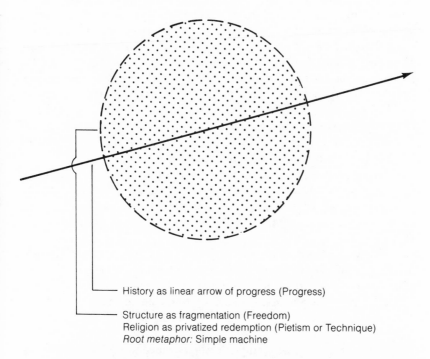

History as linear arrow of progress (Progress)
Structure as fragmentation (Freedom)
Religion as privatized redemption (Pietism or Technique)
Root metaphor: Simple machine

4. *Governance:* The governing mode of rule passed into scientific management, which tried to respect the autonomy of the parts (pluralism) in pursuit of progress, and yet to avoid the dual extremes of anarchy and tyranny. The common good was seen as guaranteed indirectly by an invisible hand, which in hidden ways was to bring harmony and common purpose from the autonomous motion.
5. *Root Metaphor:* The root metaphor is the machine of Newtonian physics, whose autonomous parts act as counter-pressures to each other and thereby advance the machine's trajectory of progress.

This vision became the cultural foundation of industrial capitalism, of liberal democracy, and of liberal culture, including liberal visions of Christianity. It focused on progress as evolution, freedom as atomization, and a dualism of private religiosity and public secularism, all guided by technocratic pragmatism.

The Modern Radicalization of Marxism: Cybernetic Mechanism

The second ideological challenge to the classical worldview, and the first to the liberal worldview, came from Marxism. By Marxism here, I mean the form of thought that triumphed in the Soviet state. There is debate about to what degree Marx himself can be held accountable for this, and how much is independently derived from Engels, Lenin, and premodern Slavic history. In my reading, Marx's own thought had two sides to it, one advancing the destructive features of Enlightenment rationality (the scientific positivist side), the other straining beyond the limits of the Enlightenment (the truly dialectical or Hegelian side). The former became dominant in orthodox Marxism, while the latter proves creative only when retrieved in a postliberal, post-Marxian, postmodern framework. [11] The dominant side of Marxism proved not a radical alternative to the liberal Enlightenment vision, but only a radicalization of its foundational principles. For Marxism, liberalism was not rationalistic enough: liberalism had opened the door to a scientific society, but had not followed through all the way. [12]

Marxism directed its critique of liberalism to the massive social injustices of industrial capitalism. In many cases, it was able to form an alliance of its left-wing intelligentsia with the exploited sectors of the industrial proletariat, and later with sectors of the displaced peasantry of the Third World.

But Marxism's critique of capitalism, as analyzed by Roberto Mangabeira Unger, is only a partial critique. [13] It hides the more powerful and underlying modern drive to further the secular technocratic rationalization of society. This can be seen by analyzing Marxism in terms of our five dimensions.

1. *Time:* The future is still unleashed by breaking with the past, but now in revolutionary fashion. The arrow of progress does not gradually evolve, but with revolution makes an apocalytic turn upward. So short is the turn that in postrevolutionary Marxism the tendency is to shut out both past and future. The past is shut out by blocking authentic historical memory. The future is shut out by a premature eschatological consolidation, hostile to authentic historical imagination. The orthodox Marxian view thus tends toward two views of history—apocalyptic before the revolution and triumphalistic after it. Science is fulfilled with a socialist state.

2. *Space:* The shattered liberal whole is reordered under the guidance of the scientific socialist intelligentsia. Again there are two moments: the prerevolutionary organization of workers and/or peasants into a mass block under the strategic guidance of socialist

intellectuals for the purpose of forcing the capitalist class off the field (a parallelogram of forces from Newtonian physics) and, later, in the postrevolutionary phase, the scientific (Newtonian) reorganization of the whole society by the intelligentsia through the scientific state.

Figure C—The Prerevolutionary Marxian Vision

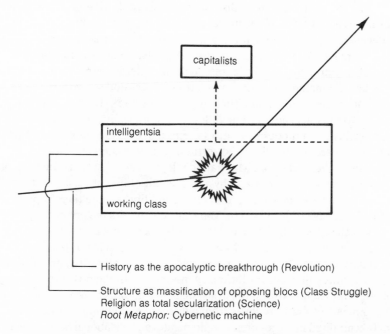

History as the apocalyptic breakthrough (Revolution)
Structure as massification of opposing blocs (Class Struggle)
Religion as total secularization (Science)
Root Metaphor: Cybernetic machine

3. *The Holy:* The secular-religious dualism of liberalism dissolves into total secularization. Religion is either totally suppressed or controlled by the state as a concession to residual premodern elements. Secular science, centered in the state, emerges as the modern religion.

4. *Governance:* Stratetic intelligence (as defined by modernity) becomes the direct governing principle, replacing direct rule from the premodern period, and the indirect management of progressive competition in the liberal form. Lacking any truly religious foundation, however, reason collapses into instrumental rationality where the state becomes its absolute fulfillment.

5. *Root Metaphor:* The machine is again the root metaphor, but, in contrast with the politically unguided machine of liberalism, it becomes now a formally intelligent or cybernetic machine. The party with the bureaucracy becomes the formal mind of the social machine. The premodern structure of hierarchy and the premodern historical condition of fate return.

The ideological vision of Marxism thus radicalizes liberalism by stressing in the prerevolutionary moment an apocalyptic turning point, mass force, total power, total secularization, and total scientism. In the postrevolutionary phase, however, it reverts to a now mechanized premodern view by stressing stasis and hierarchy in a state invested with an absolute character. The root metaphor remains the machine, but a strategically cybernetic one guided by intelligence—first in the socialist intelligentsia, then in state bureaucrats. At the same time, liberalism is dialectically shifting in its worldview toward a similar crisis of scientistic reason, although organized more around a degenerative culture than totalitarian politics. I have elsewhere spelled out liberalism's political crisis as the rise of the National Security State. [14]

Liberalism originally represented an underdeveloped phase of the mechanistic metaphor at the foundation of the modern world. Marxism by contrast represented an anticipation of its more cybernetic and totally rationalized conclusion, although less technologically innovative. Now, in the conclusion of modernity, both systems make reason wholly instrumental and consequently release powerful destructive energies.

Both the liberal and Marxian ideologies can be seen as founded on the mechanics of Newtonian physics. The initial liberal version is that of a machine whose parts are in competitive equilibrium and thereby proceed on a progressive trajectory. The Marxian version sees the prerevolutionary parts in class disequilibrium and thereby blocked from a dramatic forward trajectory. Prerevolutionary Marxism seeks to massify the particles (the working class) and force the opposing bloc (the capitalist class) off the field, thereby unleashing the revolutionary movement. In the postrevolutionary phase, however, Marxism shifts to a system held in stasis by force from above. Late liberalism similarly shifts from a diffused equilibrium to one increasingly centralized into economic conglomerates and a National Security State, beginning a phase of conservative or authoritarian liberalism. The Newtonian paradigm in all of these versions misses fundamental dimensions of the social and ecological reality, and so grows more destructive.

IV. THE POSTMODERN PARADIGM: THE WORK OF ART[15]

In this final crisis of the modern drive and in the growing convergence of the two main modern ideologies, the search opens for a postmodern vision. Initially, the search for this postmodern vision takes the shape of a turn from one modern ideology to the other, depending on which ideology is dominant in one's environment. In the communist world, critics often turn to liberalism as a source of freedom. They may do this in various degrees, perhaps hoping to shift the whole system to capitalism, or else only looking for a liberal or democratic revision of socialism. In the capitalist world, critics often turn to Marxism as a vision of justice. Again, they may do so in various degrees, with some simply accepting an orthodox Marxist viewpoint, while others attempt to create a more cooperative form of capitalism. Each ideology thus offers a creative partial critique of the other. But each critique is only partial. Each still fails to criticize itself and, above all, fails to criticize the common destructive tendencies of the mechanistic root metaphor underlying both ideologies in the late modern crisis. Each partial critique, therefore, becomes truly creative only if it opens to the wider search for a postmodern vision.

I now sketch the postmodern paradigm that I perceive to be emerging in the praxis of the Catholic transformation. Theoretical articulation of this postliberal, post-Marxist, and postmodern praxis has yet to be accomplished. But this postmodern vision is the direction, I believe, toward which the praxis points. Because there is not space here to argue that this is indeed the case, I simply propose a hypothesis. This implicit postmodern paradigm can be outlined by contrasting it with the prior paradigms in terms of the five dimensions used before.

1. *Time:* The classical view saw history as the repetitive biological cycle of birth and decay, yet containing within its soul a transcendent core of eternal truth protected by the rock-like institutions of civilization. The two modern ideologies broke with the classical heritage by turning the repetitive cycle into a linear arrow of progress (evolutionary or revolutionary) and (partially or completely) dissolving the transcendent religious core of the civilization into scientific secularization. For the classical view, the future was a continuation of the past and the conservation of eternal truth. For the modern view, the future became a liberation from the past and the discovery of new scientific truths. How then would a postmodern perspective differ?

I propose that the postmodern vision is moving toward a truly dialectical view of history as an ongoing creation. Linking radical memory (roots) with creative imagination (development), the new future emerges to challenge the present, but it remains a future rooted in the past. Reaching for the future entails tapping past roots. Past and future thus form an ecology of the historical whole. Dynamic movement continues, not as rejection of the past, but as a deepening of its creative energy.

Such a truly dialectical view could be viewed in the figure of a spiral and recalls the prophetic biblical view of history. It taps the tradition to break the idolatry of the present, thereby deepening new creation in the future. Time is not a closed circle, nor an uprooting arrow, but a holistic spiral.

2. *Space:* If the mutuality of rootedness and development constitutes the historical axis for the postmodern vision, networked communion constitutes its structural axis. The social body is not a

hierarchical pyramid, as in the classical ideology (where the lower existed for the higher); nor is it simply a collection of Newtonian particles (liberally dispersed in a competitive equilibrium or politically massified as a single force), as in the modern ideologies. Rather, the parts exist in holistic communion with each other: each part has distinct dignity, while each cooperates creatively for the whole. Above all, the creativity is in the communion, so that the whole becomes more than the sum of its parts, both structurally and historically.

Community is the foundation of the creative act. Community, in turn, unleashes its creativity by tapping its historical roots and freeing its creative imagination. The historical and the structural principles are thus linked in a communal and creative ecology of time and space. Furthermore, the communion is not simply social (among humans), but also religious (with the Mystery) and ecological (with nature).

Figure D—The Postmodern Vision

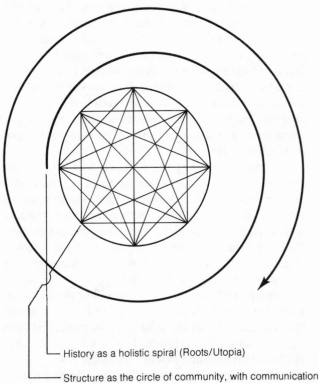

History as a holistic spiral (Roots/Utopia)

Structure as the circle of community, with communication and participation diffused (Participation)

Religion as the sacrality of creation and re-creation (Mystery)

Root Metaphor: The work of art

3. *The Holy:* For the classical ideology, the whole was sacred, but its sacrality flowed from the domination of the lower by the higher, pursued by a nonhistorical spiritual flight from nature. The modern ideologies rightfully awakened historical consciousness, although they still set it against nature and substituted religious privatization and public secularization for holistic sacralism. For the postmodern paradigm, however, secularism is rejected and the sacred is rediscovered, but as disclosed in the creative communion across the natural and social ecology of time and space. The sacred is revealed in the creativity of natural, social, and religious communion, continually tapping the roots and opening the imagination.

Formation of community, tapping the roots, stirring the creative imagination—these are ultimately religious acts which begin to pervade and transform the whole social and natural ecology. The classical image of God as objective domination fades, as does the modern image of God as subjective privatization. What discloses spiritual power is the living Mystery revealing itself in ongoing creation and re-creation.

4. *Governance:* Here we see governance not as the traditional hierarchical rule, nor as liberal pluralistic management, nor as strategic intellectual control. Leadership remains important, with real authority, as does the institutional embodiment of leadership. But governance becomes the service of communal creativity.

5. *Root Metaphor:* The root metaphor of the classical premodern period was organic (the body), housing a fortified, transcendent soul. The root metaphor of the modern period became mechanistic (the machine), initially in liberalism only a physical machine, later in Marxism a cybernetic machine. The root metaphor of the postmodern period becomes artistic (the work of art), expressed in the creative ecological communion of nature and history, across time and space, and flowing from the religious Mystery.

CHART I

Summary of Ideological Visions

Vision	History	Structure	Religion
Classical:	circle	hierarchy	eternal truth
Liberal:	arrow (evolution)	competition	privatization
Marxian:	arrow (revolution)	massification	secularization
Postmodern:	spiral	community	creation

This postmodern social and religious vision can be described in various ways. Gibson Winter, stressing the artistic theme, has referred to it as the emergence of a creative society. [16] Others have highlighted the principle of community, referring to a communitarian society. [17] Others have pointed to the end of secularism and envisaged the postmodern as a specifically religious society. [18] Others have stressed the recovery of roots, reacting against the uprooted and manipulative cosmopolitanism of late modernity. [19] Using the centrality of the ecological principle and embracing natural creation as well, some speak of an ecological society. [20] In any case, and in every one, the pattern is postmodern.

A Postmodern Ecclesial Praxis

One might ask where these postmodern patterns are found in the current praxis of the Catholic Church. Again, there is not space fully to chronicle or argue their unfolding, but I offer a few criteria and illustrations.

A general postmodern praxis might be argued from the two great Catholic challenges to modern ideologies, one against the capitalist form in the Third World, the other against the communist form in Eastern Europe. Note that both are peripheries of their respective superpowers, in effect modern Galilees. These two fundamental challenges have not been coordinated and may even seem opposed to each other. But I propose that they will increasingly converge in solidarity.

Both these challenges share a common postmodern *historical* consciousness—the creative communion of subversive memory and prophetic imagination. For example, Latin American liberation theology recalls the journey of the indigenous poor, and imagines an alternative future. Polish Catholicism clings stubbornly to its traditional roots, yet simultaneously projects a transformed future of Eastern Europe. In both cases, the new historical consciousness is more progressive than that of modernists and more rooted than that of traditionalists.

In terms of social structure, the theme of community is revealed in Latin American Catholicism's pastoral priority of the *basic Christian community* (now spreading throughout the world), and in Polish Catholicism's communitarian concept of *Solidarnosc*. Both models see that the classical hierarchies of authoritarian domination are repugnant, that liberal individualism produces alienation and loneliness, and that collectivist massification proves sterile.

The *governing ideal* of postmodern Catholicism is not authoritarian or individualistic or massified; rather, it is communitarian. The focal energies of the Christian counterculture are not on the individual or the state, but on the community. But community is not set against personal dignity in a massified collectivism, nor against institutional embodiment in individualist erosion.

For the sense of *the holy*, the core themes of creation and new creation can be seen in the rise of Catholic creation-oriented spiritualities, healing the classical anti-creation spiritualities of spatial transcendence and repressive asceticism, and the modern anti-creation spiritualities of privatized pietism or holiness of technique. The heritage of past spiritualities is tapped, but it is integrated into the primacy of the new orientation of creation and re-creation. One thinks here of American theologians such as Matthew Fox and Thomas Berry.[21] Liberation theology is also linked to this creation perspective by the centrality of the Exodus theme, not simply as negative emancipation, but as the biblical vision of new creation. Finally, the Polish-rooted theology of John Paul II gives great stress to the creation theme.[22]

In sum, I propose that elements of the new global praxis of the Catholic Church contain implicitly a vision of history as the creative yet rooted power of living tradition, of structure as the creativity of community, of the holy as experienced through human participation in the ongoing divine creation and re-creation, of governance as the institutional mediation of communal creativity, and beneath it all of a postmodern artistic root metaphor.

Although the new Catholic praxis begins to disengage from its earlier coalition with liberalism or capitalism, and to dialogue with Marxism yet not embrace it, the fresh path is nonetheless not a Catholic "third way" between capitalism and socialism. It is, rather, the fruit of a Catholic encounter with the entire experience of modernity and the exploration of a fresh postmodern vision.

Ecumenical Implications

This implicit rise of a postmodern praxis within the Catholic Church suggests also a postmodern theological foundation for an ecumenical Christianity—dialectically linking classical Catholic and modern Protestant insights.

The premodern classical vision and the initial liberal modern vision were sequentially linked with the theological foundations of classical Catholicism and modern Protestantism. The contemporary liberalization of Catholicism also draws on the liberal vision. But the roots and future of Christianity are not bound to these enculturations. Indeed, I propose that a more Catholic form of Christianity, opening on an ecumenical synthesis, is being born out of the fresh praxis.

On the historical axis, this postmodern Christianity retrieves a biblical vision of prophetic time—again subversive memory and prophetic imagination. Both Passover and Eucharist recall the past in order to move toward the future. The prophets thus tap the creative energies of the past to subvert the idolatrous present by unleashing the future as new creation. This orientation to time is distinguished from the nonhistorical contemplative gaze stressed by classical Catholicism, and from the negative historical movement of Protestantism based on a vision of the transcendence of God as the totally other Lordship of Jesus Christ standing in judgment over corrupt society.

On the spatial axis, postmodern Catholic praxis retrieves the biblical model of a covenanted community. This is different from the authoritarian structure of religious domination that emerged in classical Catholicism, and from the individual conversions (like so many private contracts) and denominational fragmentation that provided the structural model for modern Protestantism. Rather, the community is called forth as a whole, neither authoritarian nor fragmented, but communal and institutionally embodied. Classical Catholic authoritarian clericalism and modern Protestant subjective privatization are both distortions of this image. They block the community's creative power.

At the deepest level, this praxis is a retrieval of the foundational doctrine of continuing creation and re-creation. This doctrine was diminished by the hierarchical vision of eternal truth in classical Catholicism, which saw no truly historical process in creation. It was also diminished by the modern Protestant fixation on negative condemnation and judgment, which presupposed history to be corrupt.

The classical Catholic view, having no dynamic sense of history, condensed evil into either individual sin (especially sexual) or internal or external enemies of the consolidated civilization (for example, Jews, heretics, or Islam). It fixated the positive side of the creation in a contemplative stasis mediated by Christendom. Nature and grace were complementary (at least within Christendom), but both were static.

The modern Protestant view, by contrast, destroyed the stasis, but only negatively—by stressing the judgmental side of God's transcendence, thus again disparaging creation. Human nature was seen as so corrupt that grace could only triumph over it, never transform it from within. Salvation was in spite of creation, not through it. The transcendent judge was reached only by a volitional leap of trust, or by totally other predestination. Nature and grace stood in opposition.

David Tracy has helpfully distinguished these distinct classical Catholic and modern Protestant tendencies as the Catholic analogical and the Protestant dialectical imagination. He uses the term *dialectical* in a Kantian or Barthian sense of polar opposites. I prefer to describe the Protestant imagination as simply oppositional, however, leaving the term dialectical for what Paul Ricoeur calls a creative dialectic, an opposition that brings forth in mutual tension a new creation. Such a Hegelian rather than Kantian dialectic would be the foundational imagination for a postmodern ecumenical theology.[23]

The postmodern Christian vision thus represents a postclassical Catholic and postmodern Protestant theological position, therefore a truly new and profoundly ecumenical creation. Sin becomes the idolatry of the present revealed by negative judgment, but overthrown by tapping the ongoing creativity of the tradition and unleashing the ongoing and complementary power of nature and grace. The negative sense of dynamism and judgment is a Protestant legacy. The positive sense of the goodness of creation (ecological and social), with its complementarity to grace, is a Catholic legacy. Synthesized they could represent a new historical stage of Christianity. It would be the remarriage of the evangelical and sacramental principles to produce a new offspring.

The Catholic Church's postmodern opening is thereby also an ecumenical opening—a retrieval of the foundational biblical prophetic and priestly vision of ongoing creation and new creation. This vision was statically diminished in the classical covenant of Catholicism with Greco-Roman culture and negatively disfigured in the dynamic Protestant covenant with modernity. My aim has been simply to outline the hypothesis that aspects of the contemporary praxis of the Catholic Church contain implicitly a postmodern ecological, social, and religious vision, and a new ecumenical opening. The point of my critique of the mechanistic root of modernity has not been to be antimodern, but rather to suggest the need for a postmodern social and spiritual vision to understand how contributions of both capitalist and socialist modernity can be preserved, while moving beyond their destructive crisis.

NOTES

1. See, for example, James Hitchcock, *Catholicism and Modernity: Confrontation or Capitulation* (New York: Crossroads, 1979). In a similar vein is Ralph Martin, *A Crisis of Truth: The Attack on Faith, Morality, and Mission in the Catholic Church* (Ann Arbor, Mich.: Servant Books, 1982). Liberation theology is often seen as the leading edge of this encounter with an alleged surrender to Marxism. For a review of the whole question, with an argument that liberation theology in fact is not so much Marxist as biblical, see Arthur McGovern, *Marxism: An American Christian Perspective* (Maryknoll, N. Y.: Orbis Books, 1980).

2. When this essay was originally drafted in 1984, I was working out of this three-stage framework of classical, modern, and postmodern. Subsequently, I have found it more helpful to refer to four stages: primal, classical, modern, and postmodern. I have not addressed the primal stage in this revised version, however, but have limited my discussion to the historical development of Western culture from its classical roots.

3. See Paul Ricoeur, *Interpretation Theory: Discourse and the Surplus of Meaning* (Fort Worth: Texas University Press, 1976), especially chap 4; also Gibson Winter, *Liberating Creation: Foundations of Religious Social Ethics* (New York: Crossroads, 1981), 80–84.

4. A comprehensive American study of the Enlightenment is Peter Gay's two volumes, *The Enlightenment: An Interpretation*. Vol. I is entitled *The Rise of Modern*

Paganism (New York: W. W. Norton, 1966) and Vol. II is *The Science of Freedom* (1969).

5. This perspective constantly appears in the writings and speeches of Pope John Paul II. See, for example, his speech "The Crisis of the West," given to a conference of German and Italian scholars on November 12, 1982.

6. For more reflection on this crisis of modern Western culture, see Langdon Gilkey, *Society and the Sacred* (New York: Crossroads, 1981).

7. I am indebted to Gibson Winter (see note 3) for highlighting how this metaphor of the machine came to function at the foundation of the cultural imagination of the modern period.

8. See Joe Holland, "Linking Social Analysis and Theological Reflection: The place of Root Metaphors in Social and Religious Experience," Occasional Paper (Washington, D. C.: Center of Concern, 1983). A shorter version can be found in James E. Hug, ed., *Tracing the Spirit: Communities, Social Action, and Theological Reflection* (New York: Paulist Press, 1983).

9. The more noble side of this vision provides the foundation for a truly conservative critique of modernity. Its best appreciation can perhaps be found in the writings of the late Christopher Dawson. See, for example, Dawson's essays edited by his thoughtful disciple, John J. Mulloy, *Dynamics of World History* (LaSalle, Ill.: Sherwood Sugden, 1978). The heart of the conservative critique of modernity is the loss of transcendence by secularization.

10. A critical examination of the liberal vision can be found in Roberto Mangabeira Unger, *Knowledge of Politics* (New York: Free Press, 1975).

11. Perhaps the most comprehensive investigation of Marxism is Leszek Kolakowski, *Main Currents of Marxism,* 3 vols. (New York: Oxford University Press, 1981). For the internal tensions within Marxism, see Alvin Gouldner, *The Two Marxisms: Contradictions and Anomalies in the Development of Theory* (New York: Seabury, 1980).

12. Some might ask about revisionist social liberalism and social democracy, or what might be called *cooperative capitalism* and *democratic socialism.* Again, I believe that there are two sides. On the one hand, they stand between the logic of the orthodox liberal and orthodox Marxian ideologies, and so suffer from the crisis of each, as well as being caught in their negative convergence. On the other hand, because they have some relative independence from both pure ideologies, they could provide a creative historical space for probing the postmodern vision. But to do that would require a break beyond the cultural prison of Enlightenment rationality.

13. See note 10.

14. See chap. IV of Joe Holland and Peter Henriot, S.J., *Social Analysis: Linking Faith and Justice* (Maryknoll, N.Y.: Orbis Books, 1983, and Washington, D.C.: Center of Concern, 1983).

15. I am indebted to Gibson Winter's *Liberating Creation* for the idea of the work of art as the postmodern root metaphor.

16. See note 3.

17. See Harry Boyte, *The Backyard Revolution* (Philadelphia: Temple University Press, 1981).

18. Huston Smith, *Beyond the Post-Modern Mind* (New York: Crossroads, 1982). Smith's use of *post-modern* corresponds to my *late modern.*

19. Simone Weil, *The Need for Roots* (Boston: Beacon Press, 1952).

20. See the various writings of Thomas Berry available in mimeographed form from the Riverdale Center for Religious Research, 5801 Palisade Avenue, Riverdale, N. Y., 10471.

21. See note 20, and Matthew Fox, *A Spirituality Named Compassion* (Minneapolis, Minn.: Winston Press, 1979).

22. See Joe Holland, "John Paul II on the Laity in Society: The Spiritual Transformation of Modern Culture," *Social Thought* (Spring/Summer 1987), 87–103, which is reprinted in revised form herein as chapter 6.

23. See David Tracy, *The Analogical Imagination: Christian Theology and the Culture of Pluralism* (New York: Crossroads, 1981). The insight of Paul Ricoeur, basically Hegelian, is from a lecture he gave at the Divinity School, the University of Chicago, October 24, 1973.

3

POSTMODERN THEOLOGY
AND A/THEOLOGY:
A RESPONSE TO
MARK C. TAYLOR

David Ray Griffin

As discussed in the introduction to this series, two quite different types of thought call themselves *postmodern*. (Since this essay was first written, I have become aware of two more types, as described in the introductory chapter.) In the one type, to be postmodern is to subvert modernity from within by developing the negations implicit in its basic premises. Through this subversion, the modern worldview self-destructs into an antiworldview. In the second type, to be postmodern is to reject or modify the basic premises of modern thought in order to construct a postmodern worldview. Whereas the first type begins with acceptance and ends with deconstruction, the second type begins with criticism and ends with reconstruction.

Mark C. Taylor's *Erring: A Postmodern A/theology*[1] is an engaging example of deconstructive postmodernism.[2] It is based primarily on the deconstructionism of Jacques Derrida, whose thought is rooted in Hegel, Nietzsche, and Martin Heidegger.[3] I advocate a form of the second type of postmodernism, a form that is based primarily on the process philosophy of Alfred North Whitehead, which is rooted in Henri Bergson and William James.[4] In this essay, I bring this type of postmodern thought into conjunction with Taylor's. Although Taylor's thought is part of a larger movement, I discuss only his writings here. I do not deal with any of his sources, such as Heidegger and Derrida, and hence with whether Taylor's thought accurately reflects theirs,[5] or whether this type of postmodernism is given a more adequate formulation by one of its other representatives. I do not pretend, therefore, that this essay presents a definitive critique of deconstructive postmodernism as such.

Because Taylor's postmodernism eliminates various ideas from premodern Western thought that modernity had retained, even after the "death of God," it can be called *eliminative postmodernism*. It may be that "deconstructionism" among some of its practicioneers is a more complex operation than simple elimination, but in Taylor's case, at least, elimination is the result.[6] Because my type of postmodernism is engaged in revising some of modernity's premises, and on that basis providing revised meanings for the ideas simply eliminated by Taylor's postmodernism (especially God, self, truth, and purpose), it can be called *revisionary postmodernism*. Because this latter type constructs a postmodern worldview, while the former uses deconstructive analysis to preclude all worldviews, the two types of postmodern thought can also be contrasted as *deconstructive* and *constructive*. In this essay, the contrast between elimination and revision is primary.

As suggested by their common use of the term *postmodern*, these two forms of thought are not in total disagreement. In the first section, I summarize several points they hold in common over against modernity. In the second section, I lay out many of the distinctive emphases of eliminative postmodernism as developed by Mark Taylor. In the third section, I point out several problems in this position. Although the problems involve inadequacy to the facts of experience, most of the problems are reflected in inconsistencies within Taylor's position. These inconsistencies, I claim, are due to the fact that Taylor is trying to deny "hard-core commonsense notions" which cannot be consistently denied. I thereby seek to show that the criticism is not merely external, based upon an alien reading of experience. In the fourth section, I indicate how a revisionary postmodern position can overcome the inconsistencies and inadequacies of modern thought without creating equally serious problems of its own. The key epistemological revision involves an affirmation of presensory and prelinguistic perception. The ontological revisions are based on the universality of creativity as self-creative unification out of others.

I. THE TWO POSTMODERNISMS' PORTRAIT
OF THE MODERN

Although each form of postmodernity would tell the story with different nuances, both can share the following account of modernity and its weaknesses: At the center of the modern world is the *death of the supernatural God*, that is, the God of traditional Western (Augustinian) Christian theology. Because the Western ideas of self, truth, history, meaning and value implied this understanding of God, the end of belief in this God entails a rejection of all these correlative ideas. But modernity tried to retain those ideas while rejecting the God whom they presupposed. In fact, the denial of God was often made in the name of the ultimacy of the human self, historical progress, truth, and/or morality—ideas whose very meaning was implicitly subverted by the denial of God. Nietzsche was scathing in his criticism of "British morality," which thought it could retain Christian morality while rejecting the Christian God. Humanistic atheism, in which the ultimacy traditionally assigned to God is transferred to the human individual or species, is unstable. Modernity's blindness lies in not seeing that the effort to magnify the self by eliminating God is literally *self*-defeating. In Taylor's Freudian language, *patricide* means *suicide*.[7]

Postmodernity carries this process through to completion. The resulting loss of the modern self is really a gain,[8] because it is this self that has brought us to the brink of total destruction. Modernity created the modern self by transferring the attributes of the traditional (premodern and early modern) God to the human self. That God was the model of solitary, isolated selfhood. The idea that God (and God alone) was *causa sui* meant that God was totally independent of the world: relationship to the world was not constitutive of God's selfhood. This view was reinforced by the doctrines of God as immutable and impassible, which meant that nothing happening in the world could affect God. This idea that God's self-identity could countenance no real relatedness, no real influence from the world, combined with the idea of God's omniscience, meant that God had to control the world completely. God could know the world without being subject to continual surprises only if everything was under God's omnipotent mastery. The God-world relation was that of master-slave.[9]

The modern ideal of human selfhood resulted from transferring this twofold notion of deity—as externally controlling and internally unrelated—to the human self. The sovereign, impassible God was replaced by the sovereign, isolated self.[10] This ideal of selfhood, in which self-identity depends upon inviolable boundaries, has led to a possessive and competitive psychology and thereby society. The need to exclude otherness, combined with the ideal of mastery, has also led to totalitarian control.[11]

A utilitarian, consumer society has resulted from making this human self the center of existence, for which all else exists.[12] Everything else is considered to have no value in itself, but to exist purely for the benefit of the human species, or finally for the solitary self, whose meaning and identity are bolstered by possessing and controlling as much as possible. The modern view of the historical process has also been destructive. The premodern Christian view, that the world had an absolute beginning, a definite center of history (the incarnation), and an absolute end, was not essentially changed. Modernity rejected the Christian form of this story as mythological but retained the notion of a single movement in history (the modern West) which is alone meaningful and outside of which there is no salvation, now understood as economic and technological progress. Given this ideology, combined with technological (including military) superiority, the modern self has been extremely destructive of other forms of life, both human and nonhuman, and now threatens the very existence of all forms of life. Unless this self disappears, all life will disappear.[13]

This destructive drive of modernity has been fueled, in part, by the retained skeleton of traditional eschatology. By promising ultimate and total satisfaction at an absolute end of the historical process, traditional echatology tended to empty the present of all but utilitarian value. By keeping that sense of the relation between present and future, albeit in demythologized form, the modern self has never really lived in the present. In contrast with the utilitarianism of modernity, postmodernity will be characterized by delight—delight in the present, and in the infinite variety of life, human and nonhuman alike.

Seen in this perspective, the death of the modern self is not to be mourned. It is indeed to be hastened by promoting a postmodern vision that is more adequate to the nature of reality[14] and that will lead to a healthier way of being human.

Having given a critique of modernity that both forms of postmodern thought share, I turn now to an examination of Taylor's eliminative postmodernism.

II. Eliminative Postmodernism

Eliminative postmodernism seeks to spell out the logical consequences of the modern elimination of the *idea of God*. As Taylor puts it, "deconstruction is the 'hermeneutic' of the death of God."[15] The traditional deity, with its dominating aloofness, is not replaced by some less repressive notion of deity. The idea of a unifying One or Center of existence is instead eliminated altogether. A central perspective, serving as the judge and criterion of truth, is denied. What remains is a multiplicity of perspectives, none of which is more normative than the others.

There is, accordingly, *no truth*. Saying this does not merely mean that we cannot know the truth; it means, as Nietzsche said, that there is no true world. The death of God means absolute relativism: there is no eternal truth, only everlasting flux. [16]

The death of God also means the *disappearance of the self.* The enclosed, centered self was a theological invention, created in the image of the enclosed, self-centered God. As that God goes, so goes the self. [17] Just as this postmodernism eliminates rather than revising the notion of a transcendent center of reality, so it eliminates rather than revising the notion of a centered self: "nothing within this noncentered whole can be centered or whole." [18]

Instead of being completely independent of relations, the self is regarded as *thoroughly* relational. Whereas the modern self was a substance in the Cartesian sense, requiring no relations to exist, the postmodern subject is primordially relational; it is *constituted* by its relations. [19] This statement is intended radically. The subject is not understood to be *causa sui* in any sense. Besides not being prior to its properties, it is not even distinct from them. It is "nothing other than the generative interplay of properties." [20] Rather than in any way being responsible for its relationships, it is a mere function of the intersection of impersonal structures: "the subject is not self-centered but is a cipher for forces that play through it." [21] No "inner transcendence" is to be affirmed. [22] The self is thus not only desubstantialized but also completely deindividualized, [23] which means that the self has really disappeared. The word *I* can only be used with scare quotes. [24] The death of the self means the end of the self as an "intentional agent." [25]

Also to be eliminated is any *translinguistic referent* for linguistic signs. Signs refer only to other signs; they are not interpretations of some "real thing" beyond language. [26] This elimination is also said to follow from the death of God, because God was the "ultimate transcendent signified." By being the ultimate locus of truth, God provided stability and singleness of meaning for words. If no central perspective exists, however, no objective truth exists to which our words are trying to approximate. Our interpretations have nothing to interpret besides other interpretations. [27]

Although deduced from the death of God, the denial of a translinguistic referent for language is also based directly upon an analysis of experience. This analysis reveals, it is claimed, that we have no raw experience, no experience of uninterpreted data, no access to a prelinguistic world which would provide a critical norm. [28] "The distinction between signifier and signified is actually a product of consciousness itself." Interpreting experience in terms of a criterion (a signified) which is external to and hence independent of consciousness "fails to do justice to the creativity and productivity of consciousness." [29] "Consciousness, therefore, deals *only* with signs and never reaches the thing itself," or rather, "the thing itself . . . is itself a *sign*." [30] The conclusion that truth does not exist can accordingly be derived by inspecting experience carefully as well as by thinking through the implications of atheism.

Because we can never get beyond interpretation to reality itself, according to this position, talk about *truth as correspondence* of interpretation to reality makes no sense. Discussion can only consist of the superficial play of signs without truth.[31] In the discussion of the "meaning" of a text, for example, no fundamental meaning exists, such as the *intention* the author had while writing it, to which the interpretation should correspond. The text does not pre-exist its interpretations; the text and its interpretations arise codependently.[32] Hence, an "interpretation is actually intrinsic to the text's own becoming."[33]

A hermeneutic of the death of God also eliminates the idea of *history as a directed process.* The world has no beginning, no end toward which it is headed, and there is no Logos directing the interplay of forces.[34] Rather, history is "a random sequence of meaningless occurrences."[35] The postmodern person accordingly has no aim whatsoever: "The prospect of *radical* purposelessness emerges with a realization 'that becoming has no goal and that underneath all becoming there is no grand unity'."[36] The postmodern person is called to a life of erring, which means to wander "aimlessly and unprofitably."[37]

If history is meaningless, the present cannot be compared unfavorably with the past or future in terms of a distinction between reality and ideality. The present involves no fall from primal perfection, nor is it headed toward a perfect end, or even toward an increase in satisfaction. Because becoming need not be justified by reference to the past or future, it can be valued at every moment. Distractions from delight in the present due to feelings of guilt and yearnings for transcendence are silenced by rejecting the "opposition between what is and what ought to be."[38]

Eliminating the distinction between is and ought means living *beyond good and evil.*[39] Taylor's postmodernist is called to follow Nietzsche in saying "Yea" to everything on the basis of his (Nietzsche's) analysis of reality: "In the actual world, in which everything is bound to and conditioned by everything else, to condemn and to think away anything means to condemn and to think away everything."[40]

By eliminating every idea inconsistent with modernity's basic premises, this type of postmodernism is absolutely *nihilistic.* Its a/theology "subvert(s) everything once deemed holy."[41] It denies not only the transcendent Holy One, but also the self: "Nihilism cannot be complete unless the death of God is embodied in the death of the self."[42] Nor can it be complete without the denial of truth: "The most extreme form of nihilism would be the view that *every* belief . . . is necessarily false because there simply is no *true world*."[43] This complete nihilism also involves the denial of all meaning, all purpose, all moral and aesthetic norms. Nevertheless, this postmodern a/theology is said to be affirmative: rather than suffering these losses passively, it actively and willingly embraces nihilism and thereby overcomes it.[44]

III. Problems Inherent in Eliminative Postmodernism

One consequence of the radical relativism associated with eliminative postmodernism is the idea that meaningful criticism of one position from another perspective is not possible. Inconsistencies can be pointed out, to be sure, but no charge of being inadequate to the facts of experience can be made, it is claimed, because the "facts" as construed by one perspective may be very different from the "facts" as construed by another. The two systems are said to be incommensurable. No neutral or universally agreed upon facts can be found, it is said, to serve as the criterion with which to judge one perspective more adequate.

According to revisionary postmodernism, however, some universally acknowledged facts *are* to be found. They are acknowledged *in practice* by everyone, even if they are denied verbally. They are acknowledged in what I call *hard-core commonsense notions*. These are *commonsense* notions because they are common to all humanity. The term *hard-core* emphasizes a crucial difference between these notions and most of what passes for "common sense." Most ideas that are called commonsense ideas are, in fact, provincial rather than universal ideas, and they can be denied without inconsistency. These I call *soft-core commonsense notions*. Some examples: the notion that the sun goes around the earth, that the species are eternal, or that rocks have no feelings. All of these ideas have been common to members of particular societies, but none of them is presupposed by all people, and all of them can in fact be denied without pain of self-contradiction. A truly (hard-core) commonsense notion is one that *cannot be denied without contradicting one's own practice.* The classic example of inconsistency between theory and practice is provided by the solipsist who announces to others his or her belief in solipsism. Acting with the purpose of inducing others to believe that there is no such thing as causal influence and purposive activity is equally self-contradictory. Hard-core commonsense notions are not necessarily universal in the sense of being *consciously* affirmed by all people; far from it. They are necessarily universal only in the sense of being presupposed (perhaps unconsciously) by all human practice.

The strategy of a critique oriented around these notions is to show that anyone who verbally denies them nevertheless continues to presuppose them in practice. The criticism is therefore not primarily an external one, based upon an alien reading of the facts of experience, but an internal one, revealing inconsistencies between explicit and implicit affirmations.[45] Insofar as the critique suggests that the inconsistencies are not merely contingent, correctable matters, but that *any* denial of the alleged hard-core commonsense notions would entail inconsistency, the reality of transperspectival facts of experience has been supported. The inadequacy of any position denying that such facts exist has thereby been shown. Hard-core commonsense notions thus provide a way beyond complete relativism.

Included among the hard-core notions common to every person, I claim, are the following: (1) that the person has *freedom*, in the sense of some power for self-determination; (2) that there is an *actual world* beyond the person's present experience which exists independently of and exerts causal efficacy upon that person's interpretive perception of it; (3) that one's interpretive ideas are *true* to the degree that they correspond to that independently existing world; and (4) that, for at least some events, a distinction exists between what happened and *better and/or worse* things that could have happened. If it is true that these notions are presupposed in practice by everyone, we would expect Taylor's denial of them to be accompanied by statements in which they are implicitly affirmed.

Let us consider first Taylor's denial that the human subject is in any sense *causa sui*. This denial implies that we have no power of self-causation, or self-determination. And yet, as we saw, Taylor considers the distinction between the signifier and the signified to be "actually a product of consciousness itself." Thinking in terms of an independent signified reality, he says, "fails to do justice to the creativity and productivity of consciousness."[46] Taylor is thereby presupposing the self to be more than allowed by his description of it as "a cipher for forces that play through it."[47] He is presupposing that the subject is at least partly *causa sui*. Taylor's description of the self as "nothing other than the generative interplay of properties" portrays it as a purely passive product. Taylor claims, however, that the postmodern person overcomes nihilism by not accepting nihilism *passively* but by *actively* and *willingly* embracing it.[48] His claim that an author originates nothing, and that proper names cannot be attached to texts,[49] is implicitly contradicted by the fact that he constantly uses the word *I* (often *without* scare quotes), and includes an index of authors cited. He could, to be sure, have brought both of those details of his practice into harmony with his doctrine. But I do not believe that he could live, or even engage in writing, without showing that he, like everyone else, presupposes that we have some degree of responsibility for what we do and say, and should accordingly be given credit or blame.

Let us turn next to the distinction that Taylor denies on the basis of the self's creativity, the distinction between a linguistic sign and a *translinguistic referent*. Taylor most explicitly contradicts this doctrine—that our signs refer only to other signs, never to things in themselves—when he is arguing *for* this doctrine. As we saw, his argument on this point is based on a correction of what he considers a faulty interpretation of consciousness. We must now look more fully at the passage in which he makes this correction:

Though not always aware of its own activity [this is Taylor's implicit explanation of the basis for the faulty view], consciousness attempts to *give itself* a criterion by which to judge itself. For the most part, consciousness regards its criterion as external to, independent of, and imposed upon itself. But this interpretation of experience fails to do justice to the creativity and productivity of consciousness.[50]

In this account, Taylor is not simply giving us an interpretation of an interpretation. He is telling us *what consciousness itself is really like.* He goes on to say: "That to which consciousness points is always already within consciousness itself." That last statement is true, of course; we could hardly talk about something that was not in some sense within our consciousness. But Taylor then takes this statement to be identical with the much different assertion: "Consciousness, therefore, deals only with signs and never reaches the thing itself." His whole argument has implicitly denied this solipsistic assertion, because he has been telling us the true nature of one "thing itself"—consciousness. The force of this self-contradiction cannot be weakened by saying that assertions about our own consciousness do not involve a referent beyond our own consciousness. Taylor speaks not only of his own consciousness, but of "consciousness itself," that is, presumably the nature of consciousness in all people (modern, premodern, and postmodern alike).[51]

Furthermore, Taylor's book is filled with statements about the nature of reality beyond consciousness. In the midst of the argument that we never have "access to a nonfigural world that can function as the critical norm with which to judge conflicting interpretations," he refers to the "insight" that "relationships constitute all things."[52] He uses this "insight" into the nature of "all things" as a critical norm with which to reject the modern view of things as independent of their relations. Taylor thereby gives implicit testimony to the realist's conviction that our interpretations of reality are evoked by a contact with a reality existing independently of our interpretations. This realistic conviction has every mark of being a hard-core commonsense doctrine which we cannot deny without implicitly affirming.[53]

That Taylor also implicitly affirms the idea of *truth as correspondence between interpretation and reality* has already been made clear by the discussion in the previous paragraphs. And, indeed, his book is filled with statements that cannot be read other than as truth-claims in this traditional sense. In arguing against systems, all of which (he believes) attempt to master reality, he tells us that "reality is unmasterable." In arguing for an outlook that has transcended the distinction between good and evil, he proclaims that "creation and destruction, life and death, are forever joined."[54] Taylor evidently believes that these ideas are true in the sense of corresponding with the nature of reality. Taylor bases his claim about the meaninglessness of history, as we saw, on the "realization" that "becoming has no goal."[55] Again, he presupposes in the very process of arguing against it the doctrine (of truth as correspondence) that he is denying. There can be no eternal truth, he says, because "the play of appearances never stops and hence cannot be fixed." This idea is evidently an eternal truth. Truth itself, he says, appears to be an optical illusion, because "[w]hen inspected more closely, what is initially regarded as 'reality' turns out to be appearance."[56] This closer inspection evidently brings us closer to the truth. The argument continues, with truth-claim piled upon truth-claim. The notion of truth as correspondence of idea with reality seems to be a notion that we inevitably presuppose in practice even while denying it verbally.

The independence of the signified thing itself from the interpretation of it, and the correlative idea that truth consists in the correspondence between the interpretation and the objective referent, are constantly presupposed in Taylor's discussion of other authors. In his numerous references to Hegel, Nietzsche, Derrida, and others, he constantly presupposes that those authors existed and wrote prior to his encounter with their writings, and that his interpretation reflects what they wrote. And unless a distinction between what they meant and how someone else interprets their writings were possible, he could not speak of "a creative 'misreading' of an antecedent text."[57]

The distinction between *good and evil*, better and worse, also appears to be a hard-core commonsense notion, which we cannot consistently deny. I mentioned in the first section several features of the modern world that Taylor obviously considers unfortunate, such as its utilitarianism, possessiveness, and will to dominate. His account of a postmodern mentality is filled with hints as to how it would contribute to overcoming these evils. The desire to help overcome these evils seems to have been at least one of the reasons why Taylor wrote the book.

For Taylor to act with such a purpose shows, finally, that he lives in practice in terms of yet one more idea presumably eliminated—*intentional agency*.[58] And to act with such an intention in turn seems to presuppose that *history* is something other than a purely meaningless sequence of events.

I have tried to interpret Taylor's various statements fairly and accurately, not putting on them any interpretation he did not intend. But if I have sometimes failed, one final problem in Taylor's position is that he cannot correct my interpretation without contradicting his doctrine. To make such a correction would be to insist that he is not merely a sign in my consciousness, but an independent agent who also transcends my consciousness (regardless of how "creative" it may be). It would be to insist that his intentions when writing the book (to which he now has the best access through his memory) provide the basic criterion for the meaning of his various statements. It would be to insist that my interpretation is false to the degree that it fails to correspond to those intentions. It would be thereby to insist that text and interpretation do *not* arise codependently, but that the text arises first and that the intentions of its author (conscious or unconscious) provide the primary criterion for the adequacy of an interpretation.[59]

Eliminative postmodernism arises out of a deep moral passion to overcome evil (whatever its proponents may say about overcoming the *distinction between* good and evil). This passion is based on the conviction that the dominant Western systems of thought have had extremely destructive consequences. In particular, each of the dominant worldviews—Augustinian and Calvinistic supernaturalism, Marxist Messianism, and secular humanism with its faith in progress through Western capitalism, science, and technology—has produced intolerant systems, each of which declares that everything else is to be sacrificed for the truth and values it declares to be alone valid. Eliminative postmodernists are deeply persuaded that "totality thinking" inevitably promotes totalitarianism. The moral goal of this form of postmodernism is to strike a blow against all totalitarianisms, present and potential, by undermining every possible form of totality thinking. Assuming the death of theism as a *fait accompli*, it seeks to undermine any other possible system of thought that would declare what *the* meaning of the world is, to which all other values are to be subordinated. Eliminative postmodernism seeks to do this by undermining anything that could serve as a possible center within such a system of thought, such as God, history, or the self, and by undermining the very possibility of a system of true thought by denying the possibility of true thoughts. In seeking to carry out its moral purpose of discouraging allegiance to totalitarian projects to eliminate evil, it even paradoxically denies the distinction between good and evil, which is presupposed by any moral purpose. We may decide that eliminative postmodernism is as bad as the disease it is meant to cure, but we should recognize the moral passion of its proponents. Their nihilism is meant to serve morally lofty goals. (Taylor, indeed, has subsequently emphasized the book's ethical aims.)[60]

A great gap can exist between goal and effect, however, and I cannot see how the effects of eliminative postmodernism, were it to become a widespread outlook, could do anything to overcome totalitarian tendencies. It would probably only make things worse. As Whitehead has pointed out, freedom is not promoted by skeptics any more than it is by the intolerant.[61] The denial of any distinction between good and evil only encourages the cynical belief that might makes right. The conviction that truth is an illusion would only allow the distinction between propaganda and truth to be further abolished in government and the mass media. The conviction that the historical process involves no objective meaning and purpose with which we should align ourselves would only encourage ambitious people to impose their wills upon others all the more.

I believe, finally, that eliminative postmodernism could have little effect upon public policy; it is too far removed from the presuppositions of practice to serve as a guide to practice. We all reveal by our acts our knowledge that a real world exists beyond our system of linguistic signs, that there is such a thing as truth which can in part be attained, that some things are better than other things, and that we are partially free to shape ourselves and the world around us in terms of purposes based upon our judgments of better and worse alternatives. A philosophy that denies this knowledge can be a source of vigorous conversation with attendant intrinsic value, but it cannot be a guide to practice. Those who hold such a philosophy intellectually will necessarily allow their practice to be informed by some other theory, or by no theory at all—which generally means by the habits of one's society. Eliminative postmodernism, for all its apparent radicality, would probably leave the dynamics of Western behavior virtually unchanged.

The conclusion that the cure offered by eliminative postmodernism is as bad as, or worse than, the disease, however, should not allow us to rest complacently with modern thought. It *is* a disease, and one that could well be terminal for our planet. We do need to supplant it. What we need is a postmodern outlook that overcomes the problems within modern thought without introducing equally bad problems of its own.

IV. REVISIONARY POSTMODERNISM

Revisionary or constructive postmodernism overcomes the destructive features of modern Western thought about God, the self and history without eliminating belief in a centered universe, a centered self, and a meaningful history altogether, and without eliminating those beliefs about freedom, good and evil, purpose, reality, and truth that we inevitably presuppose in practice. Instead of rejecting these latter beliefs on the basis of modern premises, it takes these and other beliefs presupposed in all practice as the fundamental criteria in terms of which to revise some of the modern premises. On the basis of these revised premises, this other postmodernism provides a radically revised formulation of our intuitions about self, history, and the sacred center of existence.

Perhaps the most fundamental difference between the two types of postmodernism involves their respective attitudes about theory and practice. Eliminative postmodernism follows Hume's precedent in rejecting from theory all those commonsense beliefs that are in conflict with modern premises. Hume did not stop believing in causality as real influence and in an actual world which existed independently of his perception. But because these beliefs could not be justified by his philosophic theory, given its premises, he relegated them to the status of "practice." Whitehead, by contrast, said that we should appeal to practice not to *supplement* our philosophic theory but to *revise* it.[62] The rule for philosophic theory is that "we must bow to those presumptions, which, in despite of criticism, we still employ for the regulation of our lives." Philosophy should be "the search for the coherence of such presumptions."[63] Metaphysics should be empirical primarily in the sense of including and reconciling these various notions.

> Its ultimate appeal is to the general consciousness of what in practice we experience. . . . Whatever is found in 'practice' must lie within the scope of the metaphysical description. When the description fails to

include the 'practice' the metaphysics is inadequate and requires revision.[64]

If we accept this standard, then eliminative postmodernism is, as we have seen, at least as inadequate as modernism. Because it has simply carried out the consequences of modernism's premises more consistently, it seems likely that what "requires revision" are those premises themselves. This is the approach taken by revisionary postmodernism.

The two premises of modern thought in question are (1) that sense-perception is the fundamental type of perception and (2) that the fundamental existents of the world are devoid of spontaneity, or the power of self-movement. The first idea is the sensationist theory of perception, or simply "sensationism." The second idea often takes the form of the mechanistic view of nature. It can also, however, be expressed in idealistic and phenomenalistic philosophies, which attribute no actuality to the perceived world. I refer to this second idea as the nonanimistic view of nature (or simply nonanimism), because to have or be a soul or *anima* is to be a self-moving thing.

Nonanimism arose in the context of supernaturalistic theism. The non-animistic belief that the world's constituents have no power of self-movement was derivative from the belief in divine omnipotence. If God essentially has all the creative power, then the world can have none. This belief in divine omnipotence had grown especially strong in the nominalistic-voluntaristic theology of the fourteenth and fifteenth centuries, which was reflected in the Protestant and Catholic Reformations of the sixteenth century, and in the ideas of such shapers of modern thought as Mersenne, Descartes, Malebranche, Boyle, Newton, Locke, and Reid. All of these theologian-philosophers were dualists, holding the human soul to be the one *anima* or self-moving thing in the world. This absolute dualism between the nature of the soul and the rest of the world made it extremely difficult to understand how the soul could interact with the body. But for these supernaturalists the mind-body problem could be resolved by appeal to divine omnipotence. Because God stood outside the world, God was not subject to any of the difficulties that the worldly existents, thus described, should have had. And because all power whatsoever belonged essentially to God, nothing could resist God's will. If God wanted animate and inanimate to interact, God could make them do so! This supernaturalistic God was essential to the first stage of modern thought.

In the eighteenth, nineteenth, and twentieth centuries, thinkers became ever less inclined to accept this supernaturalist solution to the problem of relations among nature's existents. In the second stage of modernity, accordingly, dualism gave way to various monisms, especially materialism, in which the human self and nature's other constituents were not different in kind. Insofar as nature's other constituents were not understood animistically as self-moving things, neither was the human *anima* itself. The "disappearance of the self" in eliminative postmodernism is part of this development of the second stage of modernity.

Modern sensationism likewise arose in a supernaturalistic context. First-stage modern philosophers could say with impunity that sense-perception is our only natural way of acquiring knowledge about the world beyond ourselves. They could rely upon supernatural implantation to supply knowledge that cannot be learned through sensory experience alone, such as knowledge of good and evil. God was even called upon to vouchsafe our knowledge of a real world existing independently of the phenomena which are alone provided by sense-perception. But as this appeal to supernatural solutions no longer convinced, as in Hume and Nietzsche, knowledge of good and evil, of divine purpose, and even of an actual world, became theoretically groundless. Santayana showed that knowledge of the past also had to go, leaving us with "solipsism of the present moment." Eliminative postmodernism's denial of translinguistic referents is part of this development of second-stage modernity, in which the logical consequences of the premises of first-stage modernity are carried out in the context of the death of the supernatural God.

Revisionary postmodernism resists the nihilistic conclusions of eliminative postmodernism, not by reaffirming the supernatural God, but by rejecting the premises about nature and perception that were formed under the influence of belief in that God.

In contrast with the nonanimism of modernity, Whiteheadian postmodernism develops a neoanimistic view in which all actual individuals embody a principle of spontaneity. The ultimate or absolute reality, which is embodied in all actual individuals, is *creativity*.[65] Creativity eternally oscillates between two modes.[66] In one mode, creativity is self-determination, final causation, or "concrescence," in which an individual becomes concrete by creating itself out of others. Through the embodiment of creativity in this mode, every individual is partly *causa sui*. As soon as this act of self-creation is completed, creativity swings over into its other mode, which is other-creation, efficient causation, or "transition" (transitive or transuent causation). The individual's "own activity in self-formation passes into its activity of other-formation."[67] The actual world is comprised entirely of creative events and the societies they form. The human mind or soul is a society composed of a series of high-level creative events; the human body is a society composed of a vast number of lower-level creative events of various levels. This perspective thereby contains no mind-body problem of how a soul exercising final causation can interact with bodily substances exercising only efficient causation. Mind and body are both composed of events exercising both kinds of causation.

This perspective likewise contains no problem of how an experiencing mind can interact with nonexperiencing physical atoms. It is part and parcel of this neoanimistic viewpoint to regard all creative events as "occasions of experience." Whereas the dualism of first-stage modernity treated human experience as virtually supernatural, revisionary postmodernism "refuses to place human experience outside nature."[68] Because some level of experience is attributed to all actual individuals whatsoever, the avoidance of dualism does not require the assumption that the mind or soul is strictly identical with the body (or brain). The mind or soul can be thought of as a series of occasions of experience, each of which unifies the manifold experiences of the body (and the remainder of the past world) into a central experience of enjoyment and purpose.[69]

This doctrine avoids the substantial, isolated self of early modernity. The Humean-Jamesean denial of a self-identical soul-substance is fully accepted.[70] No fully actual individual experiences twice; there is no underlying, enduring, unchanging subject of change for which relations to changing events are merely accidental.[71] The things that endure, such as minds and molecules, "are not the completely real things."[72] The completely real individuals do not *endure,* they *occur.* They are occasions of experience, which arise out of their relations to prior occasions of experience and include them in their own constitutions. This view is in fact so relational as to insist that the whole past is included in each occasion of experience: "Each atom is a system of all things."[73] This view radically undermines the early modern independent self which had no kinship with nature, and no essential relations to nature or other selves.

But this postmodern doctrine, in denying the modern self, does not deny a responsible, centered self altogether. Because an individual event embodies creativity in both of its modes, the fact that it is relational from the beginning, being receptive to the efficient causation of the entire past, does not prevent its exercising self-causation before its completion. Both forms of postmodernism say that "an event is nothing but its relations." But revisionary postmodernism adds: ". . . and its reactions to them."[74] The event's reactions to its relations make it partly *causa sui.* Because of this element of self-causation, "every actual entity . . . is something individual for its own sake; and thereby transcends the rest of actuality."[75]

What is true for every actual entity is *a fortiori* true for an occasion of human experience. Although all actual entities exercise some power of self-creation, many different levels of actual entities exist. The higher the level, the greater the self-creativity that is exercised. The human soul or mind is composed of a series of extremely high-level occasions of experience.

The idea of the self is not simply a cipher for the forces flowing through it for three reasons. First, the human mind or soul is not identical with the events constituting the brain, but is a distinct series of events. Second, each event constitutive of the soul is, like every other actual individual, partly *causa sui.* Third, human occasions of experience, especially those in which the experience includes consciousness, are even more *causa sui* than most events.

This doctrine supports the partial originality and responsibility of an author, which Taylor cannot consistently deny. It supports the creativity of consciousness, which he presupposes throughout. In Whitehead's words:

> [T]he final decision of the immediate subject-superject, constituting the ultimate modification of subjective aim, is the foundation of our experience of responsibility, of approbation or of disapprobation, of self-approval or of self-reproach, of freedom, of emphasis. This element in experience is too large to be put aside merely as misconstruction. It governs the whole tone of human life.[76]

Of course, Taylor does not *want* us to have feelings of "self-reproach," at least according to some of his statements. To deny freedom as illusory is one way to try to quell guilt-feelings. But when Whitehead says, "This element in experience is too large to be put aside merely as misconstruction," is he not right?

The attribution of the power of self-creativity to all actualities is relevant to revisionary postmodernism's affirmation of a self in yet another way. If the things comprising the actual world were not thought to have any genuine power, distinguishing between actualities and mere possibilities would be difficult. The same relations that exist among a set of possibilities could be thought to exist among a set of actualities. Taylor, in fact, makes this assumption. He correctly points out that symbols within a symbol-system all mutually imply each other. For example, *possibility* implies *actuality*, and *actuality* implies *possibility*. But Taylor then assumes that the same relationship of mutual implication applies to actual events. Event A implies event B, which in turn implies event A, and both of them imply event C, which in turn implies both of them, and so on. This notion that all events arise "codependently" with all others presupposes that no concrete event has any power of self-determination by which it transcends the influences upon it and becomes individualized. In Whitehead's view, by contrast, the fact that every individual event exercises some creative self-determination means that no two momentary events can mutually presuppose each other. The universe that is enclosed in an event is the *past* universe, that is, the universe of events that had completed its exercise of self-creation prior to the rise of the event in question. Although Whitehead speaks of "mutual immanence," he makes clear in careful statements that the mutual immanence of a pair of occasions "is not in general a symmetric relation." Past occasions are immanent in present ones in the mode of efficient causality, but the future is immanent in the present only in the mode of anticipation, because "the future occasions, as individual realities with their own measure of absolute completeness, are non-existent. Thus . . . there are no actual occasions in the future to exercise efficient causation in the present."[77] Whitehead is merely supporting the commonsense fact that, say, Descartes influences us but was uninfluenced by us. What Whitehead shows is that this relationship of asymmetrical influence which we all presuppose in practice is intelligible only on the assumption that each present event exercises some self-determining power, so that the future simply does not exist in the same sense as the past. The one relation that is symmetrical is the relation between two contemporary events, and the relation between them is not one of mutual influence but of mutual independence.[78] Because contemporary events are exercising their self-creativity concurrently, they must be causally independent of each other. Because neither has reached completion at the time the other is receptive to efficient causes, neither can be an efficient cause upon the other. In this way, the attribution of creativity to all things protects the element of independence and therefore individuality in all things while recognizing the great degree to which the world is interdependent.

The other premise of modernity that is rejected by revisionary postmodernity is "the tacit identification of perception with sense-perception."[79] Whitehead argues that sense-perception must be a high-level derivative form of perception. It is derivative from a primordial type of perception, called *prehension*, which we share with all other individuals whatsoever. This doctrine, that human beings share nonsensory perception with all other individuals, is simply the epistemological side of the ontological doctrine that all individuals are "occasions of experience" which arise out of their relations to (their prehensions of) previous individuals.

Whitehead uses this doctrine of presensory perception to explain our knowledge that there is a real world beyond ourselves. Sensory perception by itself does not provide this knowledge. This knowledge also cannot be due to a high-level "judgment," because dogs and their fleas seem no less convinced of the reality of other things. This universal realism *can* be explained by a primitive form of perception shared by human, canine, and insect occasions of experience alike. The fact that this doctrine is implied by a view of the elementary constituents of nature that dissolves the mind-body problem is another point in its favor.

Whitehead's development of his epistemological viewpoint also explains the distinction, which even eliminative postmodernists cannot eliminate from their practice, between our interpretation of a text and its author's meaning. This distinction is simply a version of the more general distinction between a symbol and its referent. For Whitehead, "symbolic reference" is involved in all human perception. This symbolic reference is a combination of two pure modes of perception which can be abstracted from it.

The more primitive of these pure modes is "perception in the mode of causal efficacy," which is simply the (nonsensory) "prehension" already mentioned. In this mode of perception, we directly perceive (*pace* James' "radical empiricism" and *contra* Hume's superficial empiricism) other actualities *as actual and as exerting causal efficacy* upon us. For example, I have a direct, nonsensory perception of my own past decisions and of my bodily parts as affecting my present experience.

The other pure mode is "perception in the mode of presentational immediacy," which is exemplified primarily by conscious sensory perception. This mode by itself gives nothing but data that are immediately present. These data by themselves tell nothing about anything from which they may have been derived, and to which they might refer. They are simply present to awareness. Modern philosophy's equation of human perception in its fullness with perception in this mode has eliminated any basis in experience for sense-data to refer to anything beyond themselves. As Whitehead points out, this doctrine "reduced the notion of 'meaning' to a mystery."[80] The assertion by eliminative postmodernists that our words refer to nothing beyond themselves, and that we cannot even say that a text with the meaning intended by its author precedes our interpretation of it, reflects this loss of meaning suffered by the notion of meaning itself.

Whitehead's doctrine that human perception involves a "symbolic reference" between two pure modes of perception explains why we instinctively presuppose that our symbols generally refer beyond themselves, that they *mean* something—say, that that blue and silver shape, which appears to be getting ever bigger, and which is accompanied by a noise, which is getting ever louder, means that an automobile is bearing down on me and that I had better move my body, and fast! It is through perception in the mode of causal efficacy that I know about actual things and their capacity to exert causal efficacy, for good or ill. Aside from my own experience, present and past, I know the actuality and causal efficacy of my body most directly. While I know the actuality and causal efficacy of the world beyond my body less clearly and directly, I can think of it as equally actual by thinking of it in analogy with my body.

This epistemological account of how we know of the existence of actualities, and the ontological account of how we can think coherently of actualities and their interrelations, provides a twofold basis upon which the relationality of existence can be fully recognized without conceptually dissolving the self and other individuals into nothing but relations and properties. Revisionary postmodernism allows us to say not only that there are no individuals without relations but also that there are no relations without individuals.

This nonsensationist doctrine of perception also combines with the neoanimistic ontology to explain how the relation we call "truth," which we all presuppose in practice, can indeed exist. The idea of truth as a relation of correspondence between idea and thing presupposes that we can speak of things as existing prior to and hence independently of our ideas about them. The recognition that human perception involves "symbolic reference" provides support for this presupposition of truth as correspondence which had been undermined by the premises of modern and eliminative postmodern philosophy.

A second presupposition of truth as correspondence is that an *idea* about an object in human conscious experience can be similar to a *proper-*

ty of the object in question. Modern dualism destroyed this presupposition in relation to all "physical things" (and the resulting rejection of the idea of truth as correspondence soon became universalized, so that even truth as correspondence between the ideas in two minds was derided). Because physical things were assumed to be totally different in kind from the mind knowing them, it was impossible to think that the ingredients of the mind (that is, ideas) could be at all like the ingredients of physical things. The quality we call "red" could not in any sense be in the rose. It had to be considered a "secondary quality" which was created by the mind (even by those who thought of the mind as having no creative power). Whitehead directly addresses this point:

> All metaphysical theories which admit a disjunction between the component elements of individual experience, on the one hand, and on the other hand the component elements of the external world, must inevitably run into difficulties over the truth and falsehood of propositions. . . . [T]here is no bridge between togetherness in experience and togetherness of the non-experiential sort.[81]

Whitehead's panexperiential, neoanimistic philosophy, according to which all things are, or are comprised of, "occasions of experience," overcomes this dualistic disjunction. Qualities such as red can be thought to correspond in a real sense to an ingredient of a molecule. (Red *as we see it* is still a "secondary quality," produced by the creative power of the brain cells and the mind. But it is produced not out of wholly quality-free molecules and photons but out of red *as an emotion* which is ingredient in molecules, photons, and bodily cells as well as in our percipient experience—even if the emotional quality of red is largely covered over in the latter by its transmutation into a characteristic projected onto an external region.) Revisionary postmodernism thus provides theoretical undergirding for our hardcore commonsense belief in truth as correspondence between an idea and its object.

The explicit rejection of the limitation of human perception to sense-perception also provides one of the necessary bases for the universal conviction that some things (whether physical conditions, social arrangements, beliefs, attitudes, or other states of mind) are really better than others, and that beliefs about better and worse, good and evil, are *cognitive* beliefs which can be true or false. One of the reasons for the modern denial of cognitive status to moral beliefs, even in circles where truth as correspondence is not rejected in general, has been the conviction that moral beliefs could not be rooted in perception. Sensory perception, of course, gives us information only about physical things, not nonphysical things such as values. If all genuine perception is sensory, moral beliefs must therefore have been fabricated out of nothing (or rather, out of ideological interests and the will to power). As we have seen, however, even those who hold this view cannot avoid presuppositions about good and evil—for example, that it is good to know the truth about the relativity of all ideas of good and bad. Revisionary postmodernism helps us avoid such self-contradictions by pointing to the nonsensory mode of perception through which we learn all sorts of truths, such as those about an actual world, causal efficacy, and the distinction between past, present, and future. We can therefore, without an *ad hoc* notion of a special "moral faculty," speak in terms of a direct intuition or perception of moral values.

At this point, revisionary postmodernism must begin speaking of a sacred center of existence. Revisionary postmodernism agrees fully with eliminative postmodernism that the supernatural deity of premodern and early modern Western theology is dead, or at least ought to be. Both types of postmodernism find it repugnant to call upon this being, imagined to be the exception to all principles applying to things within the world, to patch up the holes in our account of these principles.[82] In particular, God should not be called on to provide a supernatural solution to the interaction of mind and body, or to the possibility of knowledge, including moral and religious knowledge. Feeling compelled to give an explanation of the ineluctable conviction that moral beliefs can reflect real knowledge, however, and finding that the reality of a (nonsupernatural) God is a necessary presupposition of such knowledge (among other things), revisionary postmodernism speaks not only negatively of the God of supernaturalism, but also positively of a quite different God. This difference between the two postmodernisms is at the root of their differing conclusions about not only good and evil but also the meaningfulness of history and, therefore, individual purpose. This difference is also relevant to the question of truth in general.

The major difference between this God and that of premodern and early modern theology is the difference between naturalistic and supernaturalistic (or hyper-voluntaristic) theism. This difference can be explained in terms of the relation of God to creativity. In supernaturalism, all creative power belongs essentially to God alone. Whether the world has any power depends upon God's will. A world need not exist at all; and if God chooses to create a world, this world need not have any genuine power with which it could do something on its own, something that might go against God's will. Even if the world does have such power, God is free to interrupt this power or cancel out its effects at any time.

In naturalistic theism, *creative power inherently belongs to the realm of finite existents as well as to God.* Such a realm must exist, and all the actualities comprising it must have some power to create themselves and to influence other actualities. The relations between God and the world are, therefore, natural relations, belonging to the very nature of things. God is not an external being to whom the basic principles of existence do not apply and who can, therefore, interrupt the causal processes of the world at will. God is more the soul of the universe. What exists necessarily is not God alone, but God-and-a-world. The metaphysical principles descriptive of the nature of actual things and their interactions apply to the whole natural complex of God-and-a-world.[83] The interactions between God and a human soul are as natural as the interactions between a soul and its body. Although it would be illegitimate to appeal to God to patch up an incoherence in our metaphysical principles or to interrupt the basic causal processes of our world (say, to prevent a holocaust), it is not illegitimate to appeal to God to explain certain features of our experience or of the world in general, as long as this explanation does not violate the general principles applying to all other interactions between actualities.

Because of the general principles of revisionary postmodernism, its theism could not possibly involve a return to the rejected God of supernaturalism. On the other hand, because the world necessarily has its own power of self-determination and other-formation, God could not possibly exercise coercive, controlling power. God acts by persuasion only, and cannot act otherwise. On the other hand, God could not possibly be an impassible, isolated subject. It belongs to the very nature of things that God responds sympathetically to the world's joys and sorrows. The world in fact continuously enters into God, and is constitutive of God's reality. God is not, any more than is a human self, an enduring substance whose self-identity is independent of relations to others. Belief in the God of postmodern theology provides a model for a selfhood characterized by empathetic nurturing, not by invulnerable controlling.

I return now to the possibility of moral knowledge. The concept of God is relevant to the explanation of our moral knowledge in two ways. First, it explains how moral values can exist and be perceived. It is essential to postmodern thought in the Whitehead tradition that nonactual things, such as values, can only exist in actual things, in experiences. If moral values somehow exist (or subsist) prior to our entertainment of them, they must be entertained in some experience. This postmodern perspective also endorses the empirical principle that all of a mind's concepts are abstracted from its perception of other actualities. We cannot, therefore, have a direct perception of moral values as such. Moral values must be derived by perceiving another actuality, one who entertains these moral values favorably. It belongs to the nature of Whitehead's God to be the "Eros of the Universe" who envisages ideals with appetition for them to be realized in the world.[84] Our "experience of ideals—of ideals entertained, of ideals aimed at, of ideals achieved, of ideals defaced," is our (nonsensory) "experience of the deity of the universe."[85]

The second way in which this postmodern doctrine of God is relevant to the cognitive status of moral beliefs involves the relation between perspectivalism and moral relativism. Eliminative postmodernism is correct to say that, if there is no central perspective on the universe, but only a plurality of finite, local perspectives, total relativism is inescapable. A decentered, deindividualized universe is a radically relativistic one. Postmodern naturalistic theism provides a conceptual basis for our ineluctable belief in moral truth and falsehood. The main point of this argument (which has been developed in detail elsewhere[86]) is that the preferences of God, as understood within Whiteheadian theism, are identical with the preferences of an omniscient, all-inclusive, sympathetic participant, which is the best definition of the very meaning of our moral terms *good* and *right*. To believe in such a God is thus to believe in a nonrelativistic perspective on moral issues.

Belief in this God also provides the third of the essential presuppositions implicit in our conviction about truth in general. (The first two were discussed on pages 46-47.) An all-inclusive perceptive on the universe is presupposed not only by the notion of moral truth about what ought to be, but also by the notion of factual truth about what is and has been. If there be no central, all-inclusive perspective, then "the truth" is an abstraction without a home. Whereas what Whitehead calls the "primordial nature of God" (referred to above as the Eros of the Universe) is central to moral truth, what he calls the "consequent nature of God" provides the conceptual support for factual truth. As with the moral terms, the very meaning of *truth* is constituted by this divine perspective: "The truth itself is nothing else than how the composite natures of the organic actualities of the world obtain adequate representation in the divine nature."[87] Truth is, therefore, not a will-o'-the-wisp; truths do exist which we, through our conversations in history, science, philosophy and theology, can try to approximate ever more closely. Without this goal, our conversations will, in fact, lose their zest.

Because the idea of divine omniscience has traditionally been connected with an idea of divine omnipotence which allows for supernatural, infallible inspiration or revelation, I should perhaps add that these ideas are not connected in postmodern theism. To believe that God has or is the truth does not imply that we have some infallible access to this truth. Because of the nonoverridable creativity of the creatures, God cannot unilaterally determine the utterances of any voice, the writing of any book, the thought processes of any mind. Postmodern theology emphatically rejects any return to premodern authoritarianism.

Because of the lingering influence of the traditional view of omniscience, I should perhaps stress that "the truth" does not include factual truths about the future (except insofar as certain abstract details about the future are already determined by present developments). To say that God knows the truth does not mean that God already (or eternally) knows those events that are still future for us. The doctrines that all events embody self-creativity, and that God's relation to the world involves no exception to the principles that apply to other relations, make that clear. Belief in God as the locus of factual truth, therefore, entails no debilitating fatalism or complacent determinism. Whether we will destroy our planet prematurely is not yet knowable, even by God. Whether we will do so is up to the present and future decisions of creatures.

The intertwined issues of historical meaning and individual purpose were already broached in the previous paragraph. As indicated in sections

I and III, the desire to undermine oppressive schemes of historical meaning probably lies at the heart of most eliminative postmodernism. The drastic
step of denying that history has any meaning at all implies the absence of
an overarching context in which our individual lives can have any purpose.
The resulting human stance should, accordingly, in Taylor's words, be one
of "erring," wandering aimlessly. But we see that, in practice, Taylor and
other eliminative postmodernists do not do this. They teach, write books,
and engage in countless other intentional activities. And they clearly think
it important that we not bring the world to a premature nuclear closure.
They must be assuming that something important is happening.

Postmodern theology returns meaning to the historical (including the
evolutionary) process, but not the type of meaning against which
postmodern a/theology protests. In the first place, there can be no idolatrous
notion of a "middle" of history. The world has no absolute beginning: the
creation of our world involved not the absolute beginning of finite existents,
but the inducement of particular forms of order out of a more chaotic state
of affairs.[88] Our world is assumed to be one "cosmic epoch" among others.
There will also never be an end to becoming. The eschatological notion of
" 'one far-off divine event / To which the whole creation moves' presents
a fallacious conception of the universe."[89] If creativity is ultimate, becoming is eternal, and an eternal process can have no middle.[90]

In the second place, a postmodern conception of the meaning of the
historical process provides no grounds for a brutal sacrifice of the present
for the future, whether within the life of an individual or that of a nation.
There is no preconceived divine end, except in the most general sense. What
the Divine Eros favors is intrinsically valuable experience—delight in existence. The divinely-rooted teleology is in the direction of increasingly richer
experiences and the conditions thereof. Through its perception of the Divine
Eros, each finite experience has a twofold aim: at immediate satisfaction
and at providing the conditions for increased satisfaction on the part of
future occasions of experience. These two aims are not disjoined, because
the anticipation of contributing to future satisfactions increases the satisfaction of the present. Experience is moral to the degree that those future events
that really will be affected by the present experience are sympathetically considered in that experience's decisions. This doctrine does provide a ground
for an individual to forgo satisfactions of a certain sort for the sake of his
or her own future and that of others. But it provides no basis for a total
denial of the present. The divine aim is always for the present to be intrinsically satisfying, as well as a ground for a better future. Also, the relation
to the Holy Reality (whether we are consciously aware of this Reality or
not) will not be qualitatively different from what is now possible. Samsara
is Nirvana. The Kingdom of God is always present as well as future. Eternal life is now.

All the more does this teleology provide no sanction for forcing others
to sacrifice their present for the sake of some utopian scheme for future

individuals. The life of every person is equally precious; the value of no life is to be reduced to its instrumental value alone. Because the divine reality works by means of persuasion, furthermore, we cannot be imitating the divine *modus operandi* when we employ coercive imposition. A postmodern eschatology does not have totalitarian implications. It in fact provides an ultimate reason to resist totalitarian systems.

SUMMARY AND CONCLUSION

The two types of postmodernism are different attempts to overcome the horrors of modernity.[91] The strategy of eliminative postmodernism is to undermine horror-producing worldviews by eliminating the presuppositions of worldviews as such. It does this by taking some of the premises of modernity to their logical conclusions, thereby eliminating not only God, but also freedom, purposive agency, the self, realism, truth, good and evil, and historical meaning. Revisionary postmodernism considers this approach both inconsistent and counterproductive. It is inconsistent because freedom, purposive agency, realism, truth, and the distinction between better and worse are presupposed in the very attempt to eliminate them. It is counterproductive because freedom is not promoted by scepticism, nor contentment with the present by nihilism. A horrible meaning cannot be replaced by a vacuum of meaning, but only by a better meaning. A horrible Holy One cannot be replaced by a decentered, disenchanted universe, but only by a better intuition of its Holy Center.

NOTES

1. Mark C. Taylor, *Erring: A Postmodern A/theology* (Chicago: University of Chicago Press, 1984). Taylor's position in *Erring* was anticipated by the "Pretext" (xvii–xxi) and the chapter entitled "The Empty Mirror" (87–105) in his previous book, *Deconstructing Theology* (New York: Crossroad Publishing Co., and Chico, Calif.: Scholars Press, 1982). But most of the chapters of that book, which had been written earlier, reflect a less radical position, in which truth as correspondence is not denied (48, 57), an absolute is affirmed (48–49, 62 n.21), nihilism is rejected (48, 62 n.20), the present is acknowledged to have a different relation to the (realized) past than to the (anticipated) future (51), the unity, freedom, and creativity of the subject are affirmed (59 n. 2, 60 n. 5, 60–61 n. 9), and interpretation of texts is said to involve concern for the intentions of the author (69, 77). In my critique, I am interested not in the inconsistencies between Taylor's earlier and later writings, which merely reflect a change in position, but only in the inconsistencies that are inevitable within eliminative deconstructive postmodernism itself. Accordingly, only those parts of the earlier book written after Taylor's embrace of deconstructionism are used. I refer to the earlier parts of that previous book only to show the continuities between Taylor's earlier position, which I consider more adequate, and those elements in his later position that are inconsistent with the eliminative thrust of this position.

2. On the implications of deconstructionism for literary criticism, see Harold Bloom, *et al.*, *Deconstruction and Criticism* (New York: Seabury Press, 1979), and William Spanos, *Toward a Post-Modern Literary Hermeneutics* (Bloomington: Indiana University Press, 1980). For other applications to theology besides Taylor's, see Thomas J. J. Altizer, *et al.*, *Deconstruction and Theology* (New York: Crossroad Publishing Co., 1982), Carl A. Raschke, *The Alchemy of the Word: Language and the End of Theology* (No. 20 of "American Academy of Religion Studies in Religion") (Missoula, Mont.: Scholars Press, 1979), and Charles E. Winquist, *Epiphanies of Darkness: Deconstruction in Theology* (Philadelphia: Fortress Press, 1986).

3. To identify Heidegger primarily with the deconstructive type of postmodernism is not to deny that certain features of his thought have affinities with the other form of postmodernism as well. See, for example, note 13.

4. To identify James primarily with revisionary, constructive postmodernism is not to ignore the fact that he has been claimed by some representatives of the eliminative type of postmodernism, especially Richard Rorty, who has presented his own position as a development of James' pragmatism. A more accurate view of James, which shows that he stands much closer to Whitehead, is given by Marcus Peter Ford in *William James' Philosophy: A New Perspective* (Amherst: University of Massachusetts Press, 1982). Rorty has recently admitted that his pragmatism does not necessarily correspond (!) to that of James; see "Comments on Sleeper and Edel," *Transactions of the Charles S. Peirce Society* XXI (1985).

5. Criticisms of deconstructionist writings are sometimes dismissed on the grounds that the criticisms do not reflect an accurate understanding of Derrida. Such a response is not entirely misplaced if the critic of, say, Taylor's writings goes beyond them to comment upon the position of Derrida himself. But if a criticism is leveled at *my* position, I cannot dismiss it by saying that the critic "obviously does not understand Whitehead," however true that may be. My writings have to be judged on their own merits, and I am sure that Taylor feels the same about his own.

6. Besides the ample evidence presented in sections I and II, one can cite Taylor's more recent description of a domino effect on Western philosophy and theology: "One after another, central concepts and dominant notions—God, self, history, book . . .—tumble" ("Masking: Domino Effect," pp. 547-57 of "On Deconstructing Theology: A Symposium on *Erring: A Postmodern A/theology*," *Journal of the American Academy of Religion* LIV/3 (Fall 1986), 523-57, esp. 549).

7. Taylor, *Erring*, 14, 104. I document in the footnotes only Taylor's endorsement of the ideas in this section; my own endorsement is indicated simply by my summary statement of the ideas. Although I endorse all the ideas in this section, many of them are couched in language more natural to Taylor than to me.

8. *Ibid.*, 17.

9. *Ibid.*, 23, 35, 103-04, 106.

10. *Ibid.*, 2, 25.

11. *Ibid.*, 91, 112.

12. *Ibid.*, 14, 15.

13. The concern for ecological preservation is much more explicit in revisionary than in eliminative postmodernism, mainly because the former assigns intrinsic value to all things in themselves, while the latter's principles prevent it from speaking of things in themselves. However, the latter's elimination of human selfhood provides a basis for at least rejecting all "privileging of the human," and the thought of the later Heidegger has encouraged reverence for beings of all sorts.

14. Because the idea of a true worldview is one of the ideas that has been eliminated, eliminative postmodernism would be reluctant explicitly to say that the postmodern vision is closer to the truth than the modern. As shown in sections II and III, however, eliminative postmodernism implicitly involves a wide range of truth claims.

15. *Erring*, 6.

16. *Ibid.*, 170, 172, 175, 180.

17. *Ibid.*, 14, 35.

18. *Ibid.*, 156.

19. *Ibid.*, 109, 138.

20. *Ibid.*, 133.

21. *Ibid.*, 135, 136.

22. *Ibid.*, 136.

23. *Ibid.*, 135.

24. *Ibid.*, xi, 16, 17.

25. *Ibid.*, 154.

26. *Ibid.*, 172.

27. *Ibid.*, 16, 105, 172.

28. *Ibid.*, 172.

29. *Ibid.*, 105.

30. *Ibid.*, 105.

31. *Ibid.*, 172.

32. *Ibid.*, 178.

33. *Ibid.*, 180.

34. *Ibid.*, 112, 154, 156.

35. *Ibid.*, 154.

36. *Ibid.*, 157; the quotation is from Nietzsche.

37. *Ibid.*, 150.

38. *Ibid.*, 157, 166.

39. *Ibid.*, 93, 118, 166.

40. *Ibid.*, 166, quoting Nietzsche's *The Will to Power,* trans. Walter Kaufman (New York: Random House, 1968), 316.

41. *Ibid.*, 6.

42. *Ibid.*, 140.

43. *Ibid.*, 170; epigraph from Nietzsche, reaffirmed by Taylor on 180.

44. *Ibid.*, 140. Taylor's "affirmative nihilism" is important for understanding his response to critics. Perhaps no feature of deconstructive postmodernism has been noticed more than its nihilism. Taylor in fact seems to be tired of this criticism, saying in response to one critic: "The now standard criticisms of deconstruction for being nihilistic and arbitrary are paraded yet again" ("Masking," 552). If a criticism is accurate, however, the fact that it has been repeated countless times does not make it less pertinent. A truth does not become less true for becoming a truism. If Taylor means for us to take at face value his denial of distinctions between good and evil, is and ought, and truth and falsehood, and his description of history as "a random sequence of meaningless occurrences," he can hardly complain about the charge of nihilism.

His response to the charge, however, reflects something more than boredom with its repetition. For one thing, Taylor himself, in distinction from his explicit assertions on the topic, is not nihilistic. But beyond that, he says that his is an affirmative, even moral and religious, nihilism ("Masking," 554; "The Author Responds: Taylor to Martin," *Social Epistemology* 1/3 (1987), 285–89, esp. 287–88). The question is, however, in what sense he can legitimately say this without retracting some other statements. He says that his nihilism "more closely resembles Christian selflessness, Jewish exile, and Buddhist emptiness than any simple libertinism or antinomianism" ("Masking," 554). The first two comparisons can be quickly dismissed: Christian selflessness and Jewish exile both involve a relation to God and moral norms on the part of a self-determining self. Taylor's reference to Buddhist emptiness is much more plausible. His position is the same as that of Nagarjuna, whom he quotes, in denying the existence of things characterized by *svabhava*, or self-existence. All things are empty of self-existence in that they "exist by nature of their interdependence" ("Taylor to Martin," 288). And it is certainly true that the Buddhist vision of emptiness is religious and moral in the sense that people who realize (in the Buddhist sense) the emptiness of the self and of all things become "compassionately and generously open to others" (*idem.*). It would be a great mistake, however, to assume that the abstract agreement on the interdependence of all things implies that Taylor's post-theistic vision is essentially the same as a Mahayana Buddhist vision, and that Taylor can, therefore, point to the latter's moral and religious fruits as an indication of the probable consequences of his own vision. In spite of the fact that Mahayana Buddhist visions do not include "God'" in Western and Hindu senses of that term, they are not wholly devoid of realities that function analogously in providing norms and cosmic meaning. Without these positive Eastern elements, a denial of independent existents will, in the context of a denial of Western notions of God, objective norms, and cosmic meaning, be more likely to produce the negative nihilism which Taylor rejects, with its antinomianism, than the affirmative nihilism he wants to embrace.

45. Taylor himself had earlier affirmed the validity of this type of critique. In *Deconstructing Theology*, he said that "the claim of the thoroughgoing subjectivity of truth is negated in the very effort to affirm it" (48). See also note 52, below.

46. Taylor, *Erring*, 105.

47. *Ibid.*, 136.

48. *Ibid.*, 140.

49. *Ibid.*, 181.

50. *Ibid.*, 105.

51. For an excellent development of the type of argument I am making here, see Edward Pols, *The Acts of Our Being: A Reflection on Agency and Responsibility* (Amherst: University of Massachusetts Press, 1982).

52. In his earlier position, Taylor had called constitutive relationality the absolute, and had added that the claim that it remains constant amid the relativity of perspectives is "affirmed in the very effort to negate it" (*Deconstructing Theology*, 48, 49, 62 n. 21). Taylor's later position illustrates his earlier insight.

53. It may seem pedantic and a sign of excessive literalism to point out these examples of Taylor's failure to adhere to his own extreme statement. Indeed, Jeffrey Stout, in an insightful and witty review of some eliminative postmodern philosophy, has suggested that we should not take seriously those features of this movement that imply nihilism and a serious commitment "to views that obviously self-destruct" ("A Lexicon of Postmodern Philosophy" [a review of books by Donald Davidson, Hilary Putnam, and Richard Rorty], *Religious Studies Review* 13/1 (January 1987), 18–22, esp. 18). This may be true in one sense. These "views that obviously self-destruct" are not taken seriously in relation to everyday objects of sensory perception; Taylor, for example, has no doubt about the existence of other people and nuclear weapons which might destroy them ("Taylor to Martin," 288). But these same views are used in relation to God, moral norms, and worldviews as if they were virtually self-evident principles. If boringly obvious criticism is needed to drive home the point that the same premises that support the denial of God, moral norms, and worldviews should also make it impossible to speak about other people and nuclear weapons, it is not in vain.

54. *Ibid.*, 91, 168.

55. *Ibid.*, 157.

56. *Ibid.*, 176.

57. *Deconstructing Theology*, xviii.

58. *Erring*, 154. A defender of Taylor and the movement to which he belongs could make (and has made informally) a reply to the following effect: "Taylor is fully aware that he is continuing to presuppose various traditional notions while he is seeking to transcend them. His program is, therefore, not simple 'elimination'

but constant 'deconstruction.' He is aware that this attempt to use the inherited notions in the very attempt to transcend them necessarily involves him in contradictions, so it is irrelevant to point out all those contradictions. It is irrelevant, furthermore, because the deconstructionist's point is that *all* writing is involved in contradiction, and the deconstructionist is simply bringing out this universal dilemma explicitly." Besides ignoring the fact that Taylor clearly intends to eliminate the notions in question (see note 6), this reply would beg two questions. One question is whether the "inherited notions" that are being deconstructed are all simply culturally conditioned notions. My claim is that, while some of them are, some of them are, instead, hard-core commonsense notions which are presupposed by all cultures. The defender of Taylor could retort that this claim cannot be proved. But, I reply, until someone can think consistently without presupposing these ideas, we have every reason to assume that these notions are universally presupposed. The fact that those who seek to transcend them necessarily become enmeshed in self-contradictions, far from being irrelevant, is evidence for the claim that we have these notions not simply because we inherited them from a particular, contingent culture. The second question begged by the above reply is whether or not *all* thoughtful writing is necessarily involved in self-contradictions. Both forms of postmodern thought agree that *modern* texts contain all sorts of contradictions and that, indeed, most texts have. But it is a big jump to conclude that contradictions will be found in *all* thought that ever will be. The claim of revisionary postmodernism is that, by taking the hard-core commonsense notions as the ultimate criteria, we can move toward a worldview in which inconsistency as well as inadequacy to the facts of experience can be progressively overcome. This claim should at least be investigated before we accept the notion that thoughtful writing is necessarily self-contradictory.

59. E. D. Hirsch has expressed the point of this paragraph in terms of the "meaning" of a text, which is what was intended by the author, and its "significance," which is how it is interpreted by another mind. See Hirsch, *Validity in Interpretation* (New Haven, Conn.: Yale University Press, 1967) and *The Aims of Interpretation* (Chicago: Chicago University Press, 1967). Although Hirsch's controversial theory of hermeneutics presupposes this distinction, one can accept the validity of the distinction without accepting Hirsch's view of hermeneutics.

60. As part of Taylor's response to the charge of nihilism (see note 44, above), he says that "the concerns motivating liberation theologians are not completely absent from *Erring* ("Taylor to Martin," 287), and that he "tried to emphasize the socio-ethical dimensions of deconstructive a/theology by exploring the notions of dispossession, impropriety, expropriation, communication, compassion, spending, sacrifice, death, desire, delight, errancy, and carnality" ("Masking," 554). I have never had any doubt about Taylor's ethical concerns. But his explicit affirmation of those concerns raises the question: How are they consistent with his denial of the distinction between good and evil, and therefore between is and ought? In other words, how could *his position* support socio-ethical activity? He himself says that deconstructive analysis "can never provide a firm foundation for thought and action" (*idem.*; see also "Taylor to Martin," 287). He evidently tries to turn this weakness into a virtue, however, by portraying ethical foundations as not only unnecessary but disreputable. He says, for example: "The search for foundations is the quest for an origin that insures the possibility of realizing a knowable end" ("Taylor to Martin," 286). But that is true only if the "ontotheology" portrays an

omnipotent God. The foundations for ethical activity in Plato, Aristotle, Confucianism, and Whitehead, for example, do not fit his description. He makes a second claim: "Foundationalism, in whatever form is *inevitably* reactionary and *inherently* conservative" (*ibid.*, 287). But liberation theologians, of whom he earlier spoke favorably, have foundations for socio-ethical activity. Is Taylor claiming that they are reactionary and conservative? He makes yet a third claim: "Paradoxically, radicalism becomes possible only when every root is cut or is acknowledged to have been always already cut" (*idem.*). But one only needs to look at Richard Rorty's "Postmodernist Bourgeoise Liberalism" (*Journal of Philosophy* 80 [1983], 583–89) to see that root-cutting is not a sufficient condition for radicalism. Taylor does not, of course, claim that it is, but only a necessary condition. We need more than simply his assurance, however, to believe that only those who realize that there are no roots will operate from them.

Taylor's argument as to the sociopolitical relevance of his a/theology seems to be that, because forms of language and sociopolitical structures are interrelated, to criticize language is to criticize these structures as well, and that his position undermines the quest for mastery that is embodied in modern sociopolitical structures, especially as they have produced nuclear technology ("Taylor to Martin," 287–88). These are valid points. Buy why, if the way things are is not different from the way they ought to be, is Taylor concerned to undermine modern mastery in general and its nuclear culture in particular? Another problem is raised by Taylor's claim that his position, far from legitimating quietism, "leads to a perpetual restlessness that issues in endless transformation" ("Masking," 554). Is this the same position that is compared with the Buddhist realization of emptiness (see note 44)? Buddhists have been notable for their equanimity, but not for their "perpetual restlessness." They have been notable for their compassion and generosity in personal, face-to-face relationships, but not for their "endless [social] transformation" (even if some contemporary Buddhists, such as Joanna Macy, are seeking to change this).

61. Alfred North Whitehead, *Adventures of Ideas* (New York: Free Press, 1933), 50.

62. Whitehead, *Process and Reality*, corrected edition, ed. David Ray Griffin and Donald W. Sherburne (New York: Free Press, 1978), 13, 156.

63. *Ibid.*, 151.

64. *Ibid.*, 17, 13.

65. Taylor endorses Heidegger's view that "metaphysics, or the ontotheological tradition, 'does not ask about Being as Being,' and thereby overlooks 'the *difference* between Being and beings.'" That statement is true of much theistic metaphysics in the West, insofar as it has affirmed God's creation of finite beings *ex nihilo*. But it is not necessarily true of metaphysics itself, even a metaphysics that speaks of God. Whitehead's "creativity," which belongs (along with "many" and "one") to the "category of the ultimate," is similar to Heidegger's "Being" with its difference from all beings. It fits Taylor's description. It "is the condition of the possibility of all presence and every present, is not a presence, and, hence, can never be properly present. Yet neither is it simply absent." It is "[n]either representable in nor masterable by traditional philosophical and theological reflection" ("Masking," 550). Whitehead's doctrine of God does not abolish the ultimacy of creativity: God does not

create creativity, not even the creativity embodied in finite beings. God is, rather, the primordial embodiment of creativity. God and creativity are each ultimate in their own way, and each presupposes the other (and they both presuppose and are presupposed by a plurality of ["many"] finite actualities and a realm of pure possibility). The incessant process of creativity, in which "the many become one and are increased by one" (*Process and Reality*, 21), is very similar to Nagarjuna's codependent arising, in that each "one" is constituted out of its relations to a "many," and then becomes part of that many out of which new creative unifications arise. Because God also exemplifies this process (being the "chief exemplification" of metaphysical principles rather than an exception thereto [*Process and Reality*, 343]), God is "empty" in the Buddhist sense (see note 44, above). Whitehead's theistic metaphysics is therefore incompatible with the main insight of neither Heidegger nor Nagarjuna.

66. *Ibid.*, 210, 214. Taylor also uses the term *oscillation*, and in a seemingly identical way. He speaks of the "oscillation of alterity" ("Masking," 555), and says: "Alterity is an outside that is 'inside' disrupting all inwardness and dislocating every identity" (*ibid.*, 551). This is parallel to Whitehead's suggestion that each actual thing is an event with two moments. It is first a subject for itself, and as such is nothing but an inside, as it were; to use Teilhardian language (to express an un-Teilhardian doctrine), it is a *within* without a *without*. In its second moment, it is an object for others, and as such is nothing but an outside, as it were; it is a *without* without a *within*. As an outside or without, this event (along with "many" others) enters into the inside constitution of all those new events that are coming into being. This oscillation between inside and outside continues to the crack of doom—which never comes. Taylor's further description fits perfectly:

> Within the eternally recurring play of the divine milieu, there is no thing-in-itself. Since exteriority is always already 'interior,' the subject is *never* simply 'in itself.' The double envelopment of inside and outside displays what Derrida, following Merleau-Ponty and Bataille, labels 'invagination.' When everything is inside-out and outside-in, subjectivity *proper* disappears. Merleau-Ponty describes the structure of invagination as the intertwining [*l'entrelacs*] of a chiasmus that marks the margin between the visible and the invisible, being and nonbeing, and presence and absence. . . . [T]his chiasmic structure replaces the more traditional understanding of the opposition between subject and object (*ibid.*, 552–53).

If to be a thing-in-itself is to be an independent substance, requiring nothing but itself in order to be, Whiteheadians could not agree more: no such thing-in-itself exists. We likewise agree that this oscillation between two modes replaces the traditional dualism between two kinds of actual entities, one that is a subject and always a subject, another that is an object and always an object. Each event is first a subject, then an object entering into other subjects. The appearance of independent subjects and independent objects is therefore an illusion. As Taylor says, in agreement with Buddhists, "the self, as well as everything else, is *empty*" (*ibid.*, 553).

My only criticism of Taylor on this issue is to point out that this admirable description of the nature of reality is in tension with his formal rejection of truth as correspondence to translinguistic referents. To state that "the self, as well as everything else" is constituted by its relations to other things is to make a conjecture about what things are independently of our linguistically conditioned perception of them. It is, therefore, to conjecture what a thing is *in itself*. It must be noted that the denial of a thing-in-itself *in the Buddhist sense* does not entail the impossibility of speaking about a thing-in-itself *in the Kantian sense*. The Buddhist denial is ontological, denying the existence of self-existent, independent substances; the Kantian issue is epistemological—whether we can describe things as they are independently of our physiologically and culturally conditioned perception of them (to couch the issue in contemporary terms). The Buddhist ontological denial of things-in-themselves in fact implies the ability to see things as they really are in themselves by transcending various types of illusion-causing conditioning. (Because misunderstanding is so easy, I should perhaps add that my positive reference to "things-in-themselves in the Kantian sense" does not imply acceptance of Kant's own characterization of such things as beyond all possible experience. The rejection of sensationism makes possible the rejection of this Kantian characterization, as discussed in the paragraphs in the text following superscript 79.)

67. *Adventures of Ideas*, 193.

68. *Ibid.*, 184.

69. The way each occasion of experience involves a unification of data into a unified whole does not contradict the many ways in which our experience is *not* unified. Strong tensions can exist, for example, between competing desires, between competing moral principles, or between conscious and unconscious intentions. The tensions can be so strong as to lead to schizophrenia or even multiple personalities. None of this is denied by the notion that each moment of experience is a unified whole, in which the responses to the various data mutually condition each other. For example, the methods of psychoanalysis presuppose that our conscious perceptions, beliefs and emotions are in part conditioned by our unconscious ones, and would be different if our unconscious ones were different. Our experience is not just an aggregate, in which some elements could be changed without effect upon the other elements. That our experience is a partially self-creating, aesthetic whole is witnessed to by the discords within our experience as much as by the harmonies.

70. *Ibid.*, 186.

71. *Process and Reality*, 29, 35.

72. *Adventures of Ideas*, 204.

73. *Process and Reality*, 36.

74. *Ibid.*, 154.

75. *Ibid.*, 88.

76. *Ibid.*, 47.

77. *Adventures of Ideas*, 192, 195.

78. *Ibid.*, 217.

79. *Ibid.*, 180.

80. *Process and Reality*, 168.

81. *Ibid.*, 189-90.

82. *Ibid.*, 190, 343.

83. *Ibid.*, 190, 343; *Adventures of Ideas*, 168-69, 215-17. Although Whitehead did not speak of God as the "soul of the universe," Charles Hartshorne has shown that this conception follows naturally from Whitehead's basic ideas.

84. *Process and Reality*, 31-34; *Adventures of Ideas*, 13.

85. Whitehead, *Modes of Thought* (1933; New York: Free Press, 1968), 103.

86. David Ray Griffin, "The Holy, Necessary Goodness, and Morality," *Journal of Religious Ethics* 8 (1980), 330-49.

87. Whitehead, *Process and Reality*, 12.

88. *Ibid.*, 96.

89. *Ibid.*, 111.

90. Whitehead's agreement with Taylor's tradition on this point shows that this point by itself does not, *contra* Taylor, preclude systematic thinking. Taylor says:

> All visions of the whole and appeals to totality presuppose an implicit or explicit completion that is called into question by the lapse of time. Following Heidegger's interpretation of the relation of Being and time and Alexandre Kojève's influential rereading of Hegel, thinkers like Merleau-Ponty, Lacan, Bataille, Levinas, Blanchot, and Derrida insist that the temporality of experience subverts any imagined whole and undercuts every system and all systematic thinking ("Masking," 551).

That may be true within a Hegelian context, in which the present is internally constituted by future events, so that nothing has really happened until everything has happened (see, for example, Wolfhart Pannenberg's theology). But it is not generally true, as Whitehead and other non-Hegelian process thinkers show. What stands in the way of systematic thinking in Taylor's position is not temporality as such but the absence of a form-giving ultimate reality. While Whitehead agrees that the eternal oscillation between objectivity and subjectivity, between the many and the one, is, in Taylor's words, the "non-original origin" of all things (*ibid.*, 553), he also found it necessary to speak of God, whose primordial nature includes and radiates all possible forms. Taylor, by contrast, speaks of this eternal formless oscillation (Heidegger's Being, Buddhist Emptiness) as itself the "divine milieu" (*ibid.*, 552). The difference between constructive and deconstructive postmodern thought is hence finally identical with the difference between postmodern theology and a/theology.

91. The different strategies of the constructive and deconstructive approaches may be largely based on a different sense of the needs of the time. In Turgenev's *Fathers and Sons* (New York: Boni and Liveright, Modern Library, n.d. [24, 56]), Bazarov, the nihilist, says: "We act by virtue of what we recognize as beneficial. . . . At the present time, negation is the most beneficial of all—and we deny . . . everything." Another character says, "You deny everything. . . . But one must construct too, you know." Bazarov responds: "That's not our business now. . . . The ground wants clearing first."

4

CHRIST IN THE POSTMODERN AGE: REFLECTIONS INSPIRED BY JEAN-FRANÇOIS LYOTARD

William A. Beardslee

Our present age, or the one into which we are moving, is increasingly being called *the postmodern age*. In itself, this is a negative term that sets our perception of the world against an earlier one we are leaving behind. Thus, *postmodern* is shaped in good measure by what we think of as *modern* or *modernist*.

I distinguish two senses of *postmodern*, which are related to two senses of *modern* or *modernist*. In the broader sense, *the modern age* refers to the period begun by Galileo, Descartes, and Newton, a period that continued into the nineteenth-century rationalism and scientism which are still so influential today. In the narrower sense, the modernist period was a period of artistic and cultural activity early in the twentieth century. In the broader sense, *postmodern* means the movement beyond the scientistic modernism which we have called modernism in its wider meaning. In the narrower sense, *postmodern* means the movements in art and literature that react to or move beyond the modernist movement in the culture of the early part of this century.

The two postmodernisms share a strong awareness that ours is a pluralistic world and one with many centers. The new vision arising in the postmodern world is perhaps above all a vision that can take account of our new awareness of pluralism and the problematic nature of the center. Nevertheless, the two types of postmodernism are strikingly different.

The modern age in the broader sense was characterized by a reductionist interpretation of much of our culture's effort to interpret human creativity and express a relation to the transcendent. Its single most pervasive factor was a deterministic model of reality ("Newtonian science") which was used to interpret phenomena ranging from physics to sociology, psychology, and religion. In the broader sense, then, the postmodern development is the process of breaking away from the determinism of the modern worldview. Postmodern thought and imagination can be seen in such diverse figures as the existentialists (but see also the next paragraph) and philosophers like Alfred North Whitehead and Charles Hartshorne, as well as in the pioneers of post-Newtonian physics. Most of the essays— including this one—in the series in which this volume appears explore varied aspects of the more open vision of the world that is made possible and encouraged by postmodern thinking and imagination in this sense.

But *postmodern* also is the description of a different, although not completely unrelated, style of thought and imagination, deriving from the developments beyond the modernist movement in art and literature. Considerable disagreement exists about how to understand modernism, but we can say that the modernist movement in art and literature in the early part of this century represented an effort to make a sharp break with inherited cultural patterns, and to think and imagine bold new reconstructions of the shape of the world. Traditional visions were broken down and reassembled in new ways. But the great modernist artists were still working on the assumption that human creativity could evoke a vision of the whole, even though they thought of their work in much more subjective terms than had most artists and writers of an earlier time.

The modernist period—the time of Eliot, Yeats, and Pound, the time when existentialist and Marxist thought were dominant in continental thought—has set the background from which the second type of postmodernism, which I call *severe postmodernism*, has developed. This postmodernism is marked by the abandonment of the quest for a vision of the whole. Usually great emphasis is placed upon the nature of understanding as "interpretation," that is, the view that no standpoint exists outside the flow of history and experience, so that all writing is interpretation of earlier writing. The social and ethical judgments of this kind of postmodernism are marked by the sociopolitical disillusionment of Europe, and this postmodernism is as much a search for a new sociological grasp of our situation as it is a philosophical description of it.

My topic in this essay is how to speak of Christ in the postmodern age. To ask this question assumes that the word we hear from Christ is not a timeless one, but that our hearing and the expression of the word of Christ are both blocked and empowered by the concrete and changing circumstances in which we live. If this is so, it is of great importance to assess the limitations and the possibilities of our world, so as to see what new ways of understanding and expressing our faith can arise from the dialogue between faith and the world. In this exploration I turn first to a strong presentation of the severe postmodern vision as it is sketched by Jean-François Lyotard in *The Postmodern Condition*. [1] Then I examine how the broader type of postmodernism, oriented by faith, may enter into dialogue with this severe postmodernism. Finally I consider the implications of this study for speaking of Christ.

I. LYOTARD'S SEVERE POSTMODERN VISION

Lyotard concentrates on a single aspect of our situation, as is shown by his subtitle, *A Report on Knowledge*. He makes a good deal of the shift of knowledge, and also of power, into actual computerized information systems, but above all these serve as his metaphor for the wider human situation. They offer Lyotard (who follows the lead of a group of social scientists) a powerful way of reimagining human existence. As compared to the centered self, which was a focus of creative energy and whose expressions were the great cultural products (a view particularly associated with Romanticism, but which continued still into much modernism), Lyotard offers us the image of the person as a node in a complex network of information exchanges. An isolated self is an impossibility. But, equally important, different exchanges are carried on under the rules of different "language games," so that the consistency of the self is eroded away. Lyotard reminds us that linguistic analysis has not been able satisfactorily to relate different language games, especially denotative games, which describe situations, and prescriptive games, which set norms. Direction and norms were formerly set by orienting narratives which did not have to be completely analyzed. But neither individual nor social life is any longer organized around a foundational narrative, Lyotard tells us, and most people no longer even have a nostalgia for one of the old orienting stories which set the self and society in a history or a tradition.

One disconcerting feature of this image of the person as a node in a noncentered web of exchanges of information is that the network or sociotechnological system has its own momentum. According to cybernetic theory, it works to increase its own efficiency of operation—in technical language, its own "performativity." It is almost a lost cause to try to impose some other goal upon the network itself.

It is clear that Lyotard's world is both a post-Marxist and a post-existentialist world. The disillusionment with narrative is a disillusionment of the West European world with the secular kingdom of God in Marxism, which seemed to so many in that world to be the only viable version of a forward-moving global narrative. A loss of hope resulting from the failure of radical protest movements in France in the 1960s, especially the failure of the radical student movement, on the one hand, and the narrow bureaucratization of life in Eastern Europe on the other, are powerful factors leading such a figure as Lyotard to move away from narrative to a directionless view of human existence. However, consideration of these distinctively European factors needs to be set over against the fact that *we* are the ones whom Lyotard is describing in his information society. Much of his social analysis comes from American sociologists, especially Talcott Parsons, with his view of society as a self-regulating system; and, in general, one is struck by how widely Lyotard has studied and reflected upon society in the United States, and how extensively he has drawn upon American thinking.[2]

To Lyotard, however, this is not a despairing picture. In two different ways he indicates the cracks of openness that exist in the web of relationships that constitute the person. In an appendix to the English translation, dealing with the work of the artist, Lyotard comes to the defense of the *avant-garde*. Their task, he says, is "not to supply reality but to invent allusions to the conceivable which cannot be presented."[3] This conceptuality is drawn from Kant's description of the sublime. As applied by Lyotard, it suggests that what is known, what can be presented, is already thereby evacuated of any decisive significance. Yet there is a "more" that cannot be presented, although it can be conceived that there is such. The work of art does not (nowadays) aim to be beautiful, but to raise the question, "Is it art?" In other words, "Does this presentation raise the question of the unpresentable?" Transposed into the key of the aesthetic, we see an old debate about the possibility of knowing God. The artist does not work in any trajectory or narrative (for instance, by the use of traditional symbols), but tries to disclose what cannot be disclosed and to give (in line with Kant's analysis of the sublime) both pain and pleasure in the combined presentation of presence and absence. He or she does this, of course, in the mode of shock or irreverence.

Lyotard's other opening into freedom appears in his consideration of scientific knowledge. Not having space to report this in detail, I only call attention to a few aspects of his analysis. In contrast to positivistic conceptions of science, which do away with narrative symbolism altogether, Lyotard restores narrative to scientific method in the "short story" of scientific discovery. The new knowledge, which is the only thing of interest, is found by breaking the rules of the existing language game of the particular area of science in question. Freedom of knowledge and new discovery are made possible by what Lyotard calls *parology*. In traditional logic, parology is reasoning falsely unconsciously, in contrast to sophism, which is reasoning falsely with intent to deceive. But in Lyotard's postmodern vision, parology acquires a slightly different nuance, in that it is breaking the rules of the game (thus reasoning falsely). We are not talking here about a more adequate understanding of reality, to be sure—an overall understanding of reality is what this postmodernism relinquishes. Opening up a new possibility is purely a matter of renewing the game, of keeping things from falling into a sheer state of repetition or entropy. The human creative impulse can be asserted only in these modest ways, Lyotard believes, under conditions of modern knowledge.[4]

What place could there be for Christ in this information world, in which there cannot be any centered selves, in which living consists in making moves or plays in a network of language games that are not clearly related to one another, and in which one finds oneself both constituted by and confined within a network—a network that has its own impetus toward strikingly nonhuman efficiency, and in which the only significant creativity is declared to be found in breaking conventions, whether of art or science?

II. THREE POSSIBLE RESPONSES BY
CHRISTIAN FAITH

Christian faith might respond to such a situation in one of three ways. One way would be to recognize and accept the adequacy of the type of social and spiritual description of the postmodern world which is offered to us by Lyotard (and he is only one very articulate speaker for a perspective that is widely shared). If one accepts this view, then the question is whether the total picture can be interpreted in such a way as to disclose the contemporary meaning of Christ. This is the path followed by Mark C. Taylor in his *Erring*.[5] Christ as word brings us into language games, and the nonpresence of reality in language leads us to the *trace* rather than to presence, to the deferring of meaning which is never found, but is never completely not found either. Taylor, like Lyotard, rejects conventional narrative and replaces it, as the title of his book suggests, with "erring," which means both wandering and, like Lyotard's parology, transgressing—breaking the established patterns in the directionless movement of life. Such a theology would be a theological critique of culture, not a church theology, because the special meaning of a historical community of faith would have been erased by the absorption of "Christ" into the whole.

A contrasting approach was used by Karl Barth in an earlier cultural and religious crisis of meaning. Barth's situation was different from what confronts us now, because he was contending with those who saw a meaning, rather than the lack of it, in the dominant culture.[6] Barth contended that faith proclaimed a *different* meaning. It was not subject to or discovered in the contemporary perceptions of cultural meaning, but sprang from a different dynamic and had its own integrity. This response cannot be consistently carried through, because faith has no purchase over against culture that is not in turn influenced by culture. It would be wrong, however, to regard this as a nostalgic or purely conservative reaction. It presupposes instead that the cultural crisis opens the way for a fresh disclosure of the power of Christ and that the biblical tradition has, in its own form, sufficient consistency to stand on its own over against the culture. Hans Frei's *The Identity of Jesus Christ*, a strong restatement of a theology that places both Christ and the believer in a story, is a good contemporary version of this response.[7]

The reader will have guessed that I am choosing a third response. In this response, we see ourselves as deeply shaped by the postmodern world, and try to enter imaginatively into the interpretation of it offered by such writers as Lyotard. Yet we affirm ourselves as finding our identity conferred by the history of our faith. A conversation arising from this kind of tension, I believe, promises the most creative possibilities for faith.

III. A BROADER POSTMODERN VISION

If we embark on this course, we must adopt a position that has already tried to take account of many of the shifts in perspective sketched above. We will be working also from a postmodern perspective, but from that broader postmodernism to which I referred earlier. The specific perspective adopted here is dependent upon the vision of Alfred North Whitehead and is exemplified excellently in *The Liberation of Life* by Charles Birch and John B. Cobb, Jr.[8] This broader postmodernism accepts the decay of the modern vision, with its substantial, single-storied self and its imperialistic, single-narrative history. But it does not believe that this decay means the arbitrariness of every kind of identity-conveying narrative structure for the self and the cosmos. This type of postmodernism suggests a postmodern *worldview*. I attempt to enter into dialogue with severe postmodernism from the point of view of this broader postmodernism.

My first comment is that the reflections of Lyotard help us to clarify much of what we already knew and believed. Particularly the movement away from the self as a stable, centered focus of creativity, the self of our Romantic and modernist pictures of the creative process, toward the self as a focus of exchanges, a self that exists only in a relational network, is a helpful move with which we should wish to join. A positive aspect of this move is the effort to defuse the desire for domination, which is so easily a central meaning of the centered self. At the same time, the role of continuing commitments has to be honored also, and this is easier to do if one sees that the formulation of personal existence purely in terms of linguistic exchanges—language games—overlooks the wider interactive aspects of existence in a network of exchanges. As well as commitments, truth also can have meaning in this kind of postmodern world. Even though it is never available to us in a final and finished form, truth is as much a concern of the process of interaction as is the play and modification of the rules of the game on which so many postmodernists concentrate. In other words, we can legitimately affirm a larger world than the severe version of the postmodern vision allows.

In inspecting the severe postmodern view of life and reality, a principal question is: From where does the creativity come that is manifest, albeit only in a few privileged ways, in this postmodern vision? Even after we accept the assumption that neither life nor the world as a whole operates from or moves toward a single center, but is multicentered, still the question arises: How does it happen that these centers—*nodes of communication* as they are called—do not simply *relay* the data that they receive but *modify* them, sometimes in strikingly creative ways? The postmodern problem is not the one that was central to many in the modernist period, which was the problem of how we deal with the mechanical, deterministic perception of reality. The postmodern problem is that there are *many* centers of creativity, often at odds with one another. This is masked by Lyotard's treatment because he sees creativity so restricted by the cybernetic network that it can only be expressed in ways that are "outrageous." Nevertheless, we find a common ground with him in pointing to striking cases of creativity to alert us to the distinctively human.

By its very nature the outrageous is something that we resist. Yet we must recognize that it is one of the authentic exemplifications of creativity. But not the only one! The power that such postmodernism sees at work in this restricted way is far more pervasively at work. If this fact is not widely recognized, that is because, on the one hand, so much of the humanist wing of postmodernism is still under the influence of a deterministic view of nature and is not open to seeing creativity at work beyond the boundaries of the human; and, on the other hand, because so much postmodern thought is unable to see creativity at work in any structured form. Structure and authority have come to be so thoroughly blended that these thinkers fail to find any creativity except in the outrageous, in the effort to break or to resist structure—with the result that they overlook the presence of creativity in many other more gradual or even more gentle ways.

Recognizing many foci of creativity need not imply the renunciation of orienting narrative. This issue has quite a history. Although the existentialists retained the centered self, they had abolished the orienting narrative. With no kind of coherence through time remaining, there is no context in which the more gradual or more gentle forms of creativity can have significance. The severe postmoderns are too preoccupied with the breakup of the single-thread story to contemplate the possibilities of another kind of story. A story can be open, multiplex, and indeterminate. It is true that this kind of narrative vision does not correspond to the way in which we have ordinarily told stories. But we have pervasive evidence, from quite different directions, pointing to this new way of thinking of story, and hence of the story of our world as a whole. Even Lyotard has his mini-narratives of scientific discovery, and his hidden narrative of the quest for justice. And such widely diverse fields as biological evolution and the history of human religion can best be interpreted in this way, as stories that are open-ended and indefinitely multiplex.

In the Church today, an effort is being made to counter this stream by reconstituting the single story, in which the Christian story is the only real story. This effort is essentially *pre*modern and, in the long run, will be destructive of faith because it isolates it from the wider reality. To enter into the postmodern world in the faith that the Christian story is only one of the expressions of the creative Spirit, and that it has no predetermined end, is no easy task, but it does open the way to relating this orienting narrative to others. For narrative is the traditional way of relating value, truth, and action, and it affords a network within which to test the adequacy of claims for truth and value.

What is to prevent the various narratives from simply running contrary to one another and destroying one another—say, the stories of the quest for truth, the quest for liberation of the poor, the quest for the expression of brotherly and sisterly love in the community of human beings, and the quest for the identity of a people? Often, indeed, these stories do conflict, but if we study them we find that they contain elements of convergence as well as of conflict. It is, therefore, possible to place the various orienting narratives in relation to each other. They do not have to be "zero-sum games." For instance, the story of our nation may become fuller and more satisfying as it takes seriously its relation to very different stories of other groups. If we find that creativity is manifested in diverse and often fragmentary narratives, and find as well a tendency that makes possible important convergences, something more than *random* creativity must be at work. Creativity has a valuational and directional aspect which we can designate as the activity of the Spirit. While this is not the language of Alfred North Whitehead, it is the great merit of his philosophic vision that he recognized the multicentered postmodern world, yet also saw this tendency toward convergence.[9] This essay articulates a view of Christ from this Whiteheadian postmodern perspective, in dialogue with severe postmodernism.

IV. CREATIVITY AND THE SPIRIT

Before we turn to the question of Christ, it is important to note that it is one-sided to locate the work of the Spirit solely in the efforts to bring forth expressions of creativity that are new to the society. Such efforts—whether they be directed to transforming the society toward justice (as in the creativity of different forms of liberation activity and thought), or whether they be turned to the effort to transform our vision, imagination, and knowledge in new and creative ways—such efforts must be in the center of our understanding of the work of the Spirit. But a closely related, and often neglected, phase of the Spirit's presence is the process of growth of the individual person—what the Greeks called *paideia*, or the acquisition of culture, and what we, in a more restricted term, speak of as education. Education is a backward-looking as well as a forward-looking task because it involves the person's interacting with a heritage. It may also be a long and painful process. One of Eudora Welty's characters says that it took her until her middle years to know "how deep were the complexities of the everyday, of the family, what caves were in the mountains, what blocked chambers, and what crystal rivers that had not yet seen the light." [10] We should look for the work of the Spirit in the growing awareness of and ability to respond to these complexities, as well as in the larger-scale processes which more obviously shape our common life. In such ways as these we need to expand the postmodern vision.

But the postmodern vision, even in its severe form, has much to teach us as well. Most importantly we need to confront the way in which the system or network sets limits to our transformation, as Lyotard so clearly portrays the situation. We all know the end to which a self-regulating technological system will bring us—the premature end of life in earth. We rightly affirm a different vision, but our dialogue partner can help us to see the difficulty of the task.

We need not only effort and commitment—although these we need in far greater depth than they are readily visible; we need better clues about what we do. The general line is clear enough. In contrast to the monolithic self-regulating system presented by Lyotard, we need to recognize and activate smaller networks, which can undertake specific tasks and which can give expression to aspects of our humanness as well as a purchase for the transformation of the larger network.

Birch and Cobb see this clearly, and they offer some helpful suggestions. They strive to emphasize decentralization and decision-making by persons who participate in a particular aspect of the life of society. They point out, as well, the shortcomings of both capitalist and Marxist economics, which are usually taken to be the only alternatives. But decentralized, cooperative economic and social procedures are not doing particularly well in our society. I believe that this is as much because we do not have the theory, the understanding, of what will work, as because of social rigidities. One of the exciting Christian intellectual tasks of today lies exactly at this point. Developing the needed theory is not a uniquely Christian task but one that is particularly appropriate from the point of view of the Christian vision and commitments.

This is the postmodern world, a world of networks of exchange, without an empirical center or a predetermined goal, but a world in which the Spirit is active, leading us toward a more human, less dominative, more liberated life, and a world in which the pressing issues seem to be largely immanent and practical. What roles does or can Christ play in this postmodern world? Is the specific profile of human meaning—or rather the particular bundle of related profiles of human meaning—that is associated with the image of Christ valid or important as giving a concrete, historical direction to the activities of the Spirit? We affirm the activity of the Spirit, a Spirit distributed throughout this noncentered, postmodern world, a Spirit that is expressed in creativity breaking the established forms so that new expressions may appear, a Spirit that is also concerned for valuation (not all that is new is good), and a Spirit that is seen in the network of relationships which sustains and makes possible creative acts. Does this Spirit still need to be associated with Christ?

V. THE SPIRIT AND CHRIST

Let us address this question by looking back to the period of Christian origins. Parts of the postmodern perspective will help us to relate what has actually been going on in biblical studies to the theological tradition, which is too often remote from biblical studies.

In the Christian intepretation of faith, Christ is the image around which all aspects of reality come into focus. Early Christianity moved quickly in this direction. [11] In doing so, the early Church masked the diversity of the ingredients that went into the image, although they were quite right in affirming that the new faith was a new "historical emergent"—in our terms, something that could not possibly have been predicted. Let us first look at the diversity of the ingredients. To do so I have only to refer to the recent reactivation of the history-of-religions studies of early Christianity. A number of important works take the general line of showing how the various liturgical, ethical, and theological aspects of the different forms of early Christianity functioned very similarly to analogous structures in the other faiths of this period, whether Jewish or Hellenistic (itself a distinction that these studies call into question). [12] Somehow these microelements, when they were put together, effected a major historical emergence, at the center of which was the image of Christ. Moving from our previous discussion, we thus assert that the Spirit was active in countless microevents, which were symbolically elevated to major transforming power in the figure of Christ. I call this a *distributive Christology*. It is a modification, of course, of the old logos Christology.

To clarify, let me draw an analogy to the work of Norman K. Gottwald on the formative period of the Hebrew Scriptures. [13] Gottwald's proposal is that during the Joshua-Judges period the Hebrews established a radically egalitarian society, which stood in sharp contrast to the hierarchical, authoritarian societies of the environing Canaanite culture. The stories of Moses, the Exodus, and the wanderings symbolically present God's

establishment of this egalitarian society. [14] The real action was in the countless, nameless deeds of courage, resistance, and affirmation of common
humanity that took place as the Hebrews forged the alliance of the tribes
during the period of the tribal federation. That was where, in our language,
the Spirit was at work in the microevents (although Gottwald largely restricts
himself to a strictly sociological analysis). [15] In their liturgy and symbolic
memory, the activity of the Spirit was transferred from the microscale to
the macroscale in the great stories of deliverance.

The analogy to the distributive Christology that is demanded by current study of the New Testament is not exact. Gottwald can concentrate on
only one kind of transformation—that toward an egalitarian society. The
Hebrew Scriptures are by no means a single-issue collection; but other issues,
such as those raised by the book of Job, can be deferred because they come
at a later period. In the New Testament, by contrast, everything is happening at once, so to speak. This means that we have to look for the activity
of the Spirit in a number of disparate areas and kinds of activity. The
resulting historical process is not a single strand, but a complex interweaving of related trajectories. Mark and John may have had a source in common, but their creativity moves in different directions. Matthew and Luke
share a concern for the Christian community, but in different ways. Yet many
of the creative acts out of which Christianity emerged were taking place in
the work of these writers and their communities. Regardless how far back
we go, multiple strands are found. An older model traced them all back to
a unity in Jesus.

But even in Jesus we see the interweaving of varied strands of creativity.
On the one hand, Jesus was a wandering charismatic who challenged the
established religion and social structure. The cleansing of the Temple and
the manner of his death are inescapable clues to this side of his story. Reading
Jesus from these clues alone one finds Jesus the liberation preacher—
persuasively argued, for instance, by George Pixley. [16] On the other hand,
the healings are most naturally understood in the frame of making life more
whole in the difficult present. Gerd Theissen notes how unusual it was for
Jesus to combine these two worlds. [17] Some readers see the words about
nonresistance as the central clue, and find a pacifist Jesus. [18] The parables
as read by Funk, Crossan, and James Breech erase the sociopolitical concern and deal with the fracturing of the individual person's world to lay
her or him open to grace, to the unexpectedness of the gift of life. [19]

No doubt these different phases of Jesus' activity were symbolically
united by him around the image of the Kingdom of God. But if we were
to treat each one as a language game, they would be as difficult to unify
as the modern activities that Lyotard has in mind.

Other aspects of the wider picture are equally well known. If we look
in the dynamic of early Christianity for a Spirit of creativity and transformation, which renews motifs from the Hebrew Scriptures and opens itself
to aspects of its contemporary culture that can blend with these to open

the way for an inclusive, open, humanly interreactive society, we also recognize the Spirit in parallel forms in Judaism, with which Christianity was often in rather acerbic debate. Not only so, but if we see, for instance, one of the significant aspects of early Christianity to be that it was in good part more open to the full participation of women than were many of the other groups of the period, we also recognize the work of the Spirit in those aspects of Hellenistic-Roman society that made it possible for some women to have greater freedom—a locus of the Spirit's activity that has not been given attention in traditional theology.

Thus, the early Christian world discloses itself as very similar to ours. The work of the Spirit is to be seen distributively, for the most part in microterms, and for Christians this activity was symbolically united and enlarged in the figure of Christ. To them, Jesus of Nazareth so fully represented the transforming power of God that he was identified with the expected deliverer-figure, the Messiah or Christ; the Christ figure also was elevated to be a focused representation of divine presence and eventually an aspect of divinity. In part because of this focusing and enlarging as a witness to the Spirit's activity, Christianity and the Christ became a major transforming force in the late ancient world—one that on the whole was liberating, although with very uneven results.

This judgment can stand only if the creation of a new style of social organization, the Church, is regarded as liberating and humanizing. Despite its rigidity and the loss, for instance, of initial movements toward the liberation of women, despite the controversies with Judaism and the intramural controversies in the Church, and despite the increasing accommodation to the environment, I would judge that Christ was a powerfully, if unevenly, liberating figure in ancient Christianity. The movement originating with Jesus, gathering a diverse bundle of concerns, giving dignity to the individual person's life both by giving him or her a place in a new social group and by proclaiming the weight of that person's significance before God, became a powerful if flawed renewing force in the ancient world.

VI. CHRIST IN THE POSTMODERN WORLD

Now we return to the present and to the meaning of Christ in the postmodern world. If it is appropriate to begin, as we did, by looking at the factors in this world that generate hope by thinking in general terms about the activity of the Spirit, what is to be added by focusing on the specific image of Christ or the memory of Jesus? If we find as well that the activity of the Spirit in early Christianity was distributed among many centers and many acts of creativity, which were drawn together into the image of Christ, does this image have sufficient unity to function today?

The first thing to see is that, while the Spirit is active in many ways that have nothing to do with human language or symbolism, in those aspects of our life together on this planet that do depend on language and symbolism, the Spirit is mute if it cannot work through appropriate symbols. We are far from being as enclosed in language as some would tell us, yet the Spirit is not free simply to speak directly to us, at least to our conscious selves.[20] That is, the direct presence of the Spirit in our experiences must be given comprehensible form through language and symbolism before the Spirit's transforming power can be an inspiring part of our conscious, and even to a large degree of our unconscious, life. This is one great reason why the Spirit is not evident to so many today—because the Spirit is in fact mute insofar as no appropriate language is available through which she can speak to us. That does not mean that the Spirit will be wholly without effect, but that we will only dimly apprehend the directions in which the Spirit is leading us. If the image of Christ can be a vital symbolic focus for the activity of the Spirit, it will thus be a major gift in dealing with the difficult world which we have sketched. The question is in large measure a pragmatic one: Does this biblically-rooted image still disclose the power of transformation that Christians have previously found in it?

A first answer would be: "Yes, it, along with several others, functions well." To answer this way would be to defuse the well-established Christian tradition of making this decision the sole determining one for the whole structure of one's existence. In a pluralistic world, we do not claim the exclusive presence of the Spirit in Christ that Christians have sometimes affirmed.[21] One way to answer the question would therefore be, essentially, to cool it: "No big deal; it is a good symbolism: use it when it fits, when it is appropriate." There is much value in this approach, even though it runs directly counter to so much of the theology that we have been taught. For many purposes this answer works well. For example, consider the case of Margaret Mead, who gave a great deal of her time to Church causes, especially to commissions of the National Council of Churches and the World Council of Churches. This aspect of her career was sketched by Roger Shinn in an article in *Christianity and Crisis* not long after her death.[22] If I were a pastor, I would be working hard to get people to take part in the work of the Church on these terms. Or think of the students who attend seminary to study the ministry and end up teaching film or being social workers in a hospital. Most of them do not experience these changes as shifts in their fundamental commitment; rather, they have found more effective ways of doing what they are called to do, using symbols that are related to the Christ image but in which Christ is not explicit.

But I expect that the emphasis is usually somewhat different among those whose vocational journey runs the other way. I am thinking of the fact that seminaries everywhere in the United States are receiving a rising percentage of students who have tried some other vocation and then, later, are drawn to the ministry. Such students, I suspect, will be searching to find a more sharply profiled image of Christ, a function for Christ that is not quite so optional.

A way to this more sharply profiled image is to recognize more fully our limits as historical beings. To choose to enter the orbit of the explicit Christ image is to choose a place, not a place to stand—for we can never simply stand—but a place within which to move. To open oneself to the specific Christ symbolism is to move into the Christian Church. Sometimes this can be in the sense that "this is too valuable to leave to those who want to use it in the wrong way." Elisabeth Schüssler Fiorenza takes this view, in part, in her important books, *In Memory of Her* and *Bread, Not Stone*.[23] To express an open relationship to the Scripture, she calls the Bible a historical prototype, not an eternal archetype.[24] This means that historically we come from the story it records, and it tells of the breakthroughs of the work of the Spirit that are foundational for us, but nothing in it is forced upon us literally in its given form. Appropriating our heritage does not have to be the stance only of those for whom this already was a heritage waiting to be appropriated. It can also be adopted by those who find this the path to liberation.

If the cluster of images that we call Christ is to be compelling in the postmodern age, therefore, it will be in the context of the particular historical community, the Church, that lives out of that heritage. To affirm the contemporaneity of Christ is to affirm the viability of the Church in at least some one of its lines of development. This does not mean that any form of the Church will be found adequate to express the meaning of Christ, but that unless there is some viable community, the image of Christ will become so diffuse that it will not have significant directing power.[25]

At the same time, we must recognize that Christ has become problematic in a way that I for one could never have anticipated. There are those who find Christ language unwelcome, perhaps even unacceptable, because the term *Christ*, midway between *Jesus* and *God*, tends to impart male gender to God (or at least to one person of the Trinity), through Jesus' having been male. We have to listen seriously to this kind of rejection of our traditional language and to the proposal that we not speak of Christ but only of the Spirit and Jesus. This practice would inevitably entail some loss, and this revision of our vocabulary would, in the foreseeable future, probably be only one form of Christian speech. But it might be an important linguistic venture. I am hence suggesting that even those who are drawn by the Spirit to the cluster of meaning that we call Christ might cast about for another way of speaking about this meaning.

Thus far, the discussion of the contemporary meaning of Christ has been cast in pragmatic terms: What would or does the image of Christ do for us? I see this as an appropriate way into the question. After all, if Christ were to be experienced as repressive, one would not want to remain bound to Christ, and that has been the experience of many modern people. I have tried to sketch the broad outlines of a way of opening oneself to the Spirit of God at work in the story that comes from Jesus, that is, a way of opening oneself to Christ that is freeing and hope-giving in that it brings together those elements of challenge (and even, as we saw earlier, outrage) and those elements of sustenance and flexible structure which nurture community and human transformation. A Christian community focused upon and living from this mode of presence of the Spirit can and (I venture to say) will be a strong factor in the seeking and finding of those patterns that will resist the technological cybernetization of life, encourage cooperative ventures and smaller networks within the overall society, and help to reconstitute the story of our common life in such a way that it gives up its imperialistic claims (whether of tribe or nation or religious group, as well as its imperialistic claims upon the fabric of the earth) and opens the way to seek common values or at least coordinated values within the human community.

But we cannot leave the question with a simply pragmatic evaluation. One of the perennial meanings of the figure of Christ has been the way in which it has led people to reach beyond a simply pragmatic assessment of their lives. To illustrate, let us think of the two central actions in the story of Jesus, for these give us an entry into aspects of God's dealing with the world which we can glimpse even if we cannot wholly comprehend them. These actions, the climax of the story of Jesus, have repeatedly shown their power of opening to us dimensions that are beyond our daily common concerns, and these dimensions can make a tremendous difference in how we engage in those daily concerns, even though we do not come to these actions for pragmatic reasons.

Easter and the story of the resurrection of Jesus tell us that our commitment to hope has a dimension that reaches beyond whatever community could be built in our human society. Our deepest insight into the meaning of this hope is open to us in our care for another human being. As Gabriel Marcel put it, "To love a being is to say, 'Thou shalt not die.'"[26] This other matters! And matters to God! The resurrection story implies that the existence of the person is received—in some other form—into God's presence. It may be that Whitehead's doctrine of the preservation of experience in the "consequent nature of God" is the adequate expression of this faith in our time. However, I believe that the traditional view, that God empowers our existences to continue in some form of new life after death, is one of those glimpses that faith affords us, and I do not see this faith as escapist, but as empowering action on behalf of immeasurably precious beings.[27] I am not impressed by the efforts to offer evidence of communication with those who have died, nor do I offer this faith as a remedy to the injustices of the world. I believe that the resurrection of Jesus was affirmed in faith by those whose lives were deeply sensitized to the guidance of God's Spirit by their association with Jesus and by the traumatic experience of his death; and just as then, this faith opens one to the worth and dignity of human life, which is capable of such a transformation into the presence of God.

If the resurrection helps us to affirm the profound worth of the person, who matters to God, the crucifixion story works the other way around, and gives us a glimpse of the opposite insight, that persons exist in a web of relationships which may call for going beyond the wholeness of the person. We could explore this idea from the point of view of self-transcendence and say with Martin J. Buss that "self transcendence is an integral part of selfhood," or in simple language that giving and commitment to others is the way of life.[28] I believe this, although I also recognize the justified protests that are made when the emphasis on self-sacrificial self-transcendence is loaded upon a particular part of the community, say, on women.

I want to make a different point, however, which is that the cross of Jesus Christ opens our eyes to the way in which something other than the pragmatic question is of final concern. To make the point, and to make it for those who believe strongly that faith leads to wholeness, let me (with perhaps a touch of the outrageous) quote from a great antimodern, John Henry Newman: "There are wounds of the spirit which never close, and are intended in God's mercy to bring us ever nearer to him, and to prevent us from leaving him, by their very perpetuity."[29] If the resurrection shows us the infinite worth of the other, the crucifixion gives us a glimpse of something that transforms without removing our difficulties. Let me close with a commentary on this particular Christian imagery by quoting from a great Jewish interpreter of the Hebrew Scriptures, Martin Buber. He rendered the words of the Lord to Moses in Exodus 3:14 in this way: "I shall be there as I shall be there."[30] So, even in the cross, "I shall be there as I shall be there, even there."[31]

NOTES

1. Jean-François Lyotard, *The Post-Modern Condition: A Report on Knowledge*, trans. Geoff Bennington and Brian Massumi (Vol. 10 of "Theory and History of Literature") (Minneapolis: University of Minnesota Press, 1984).

2. We cannot here compare Lyotard's work with that of French deconstructionists such as Jacques Derrida or American thinkers such as Richard Rorty.

3. Lyotard, *The Post-Modern Condition*, 81.

4. Lyotard also recognizes the place for less focused expressions of creativity and freedom, in part at least in response to the sharply-profiled forms sketched in the text of his book. In *Newsweek*, April 22, 1985, in connection with an art exhibit he planned at the Pompidou Center in Paris, Lyotard observed: "We wanted to show that the world is not evolving toward greater clarity and simplicity, but rather toward a new degree of complexity in which the individual may feel very lost but in which he can in fact become more free" (80). It is worth noting that here Lyotard employs narrative language ("evolving") of a sort, which could open up a further range of dialogue.

5. Mark C. Taylor, *Erring: A Postmodern A/theology* (Chicago: University of Chicago Press, 1984). Taylor's work is, in part, a theological application of the work of Jacques Derrida, and is analyzed by David Griffin in this volume.

6. Karl Barth, *The Epistle to the Romans*, trans. Edwyn C. Hoskyns (London: Oxford University Press, 1933).

7. Hans Frei, *The Identity of Jesus Christ: The Hermeneutical Bases of Dogmatic Theology* (Philadelphia: Fortress Press, 1975).

8. Charles Birch and John B. Cobb, Jr., *The Liberation of Life: From the Cell to the Community* (Cambridge: Cambridge University Press, 1981).

9. For a brief interpretation of Whitehead's thought that makes this point explicit, see Michael Welker, "Whiteheads Vergottung der Welt" (with an English summary), Harald Holz and Ernest Wolf-Gazo, eds., *Whitehead and the Idea of Process* (Freiburg: Karl Alber, 1984), 249–72.

10. Ellen Fairchild in Eudora Welty, *Delta Wedding* (New York: Harcourt, Brace, & World, 1945), 157.

11. See Reginald Fuller, *The Foundations of New Testament Christology* (New York: Scribner's, 1965).

12. We may cite as example the work of Hans Dieter Betz on literary forms in the New Testament and that of Wayne A. Meeks on New Testament social organization. See Hans Dieter Betz, *Der Apostel Paulus und die sokratische Tradition: Eine exegetische Untersuchung zu seiner "Apologie" 2 Korinther 10–13* (Vol. 45 of "Beiträge zur historischen Theologie") (Tübingen: Mohr, 1972), and *Galatians: A Commentary on Paul's Letter to the Churches in Galatia* ("Hermeneia") (Philadelphia: Fortress Press, 1979); and Wayne A. Meeks, *The First Urban Christians: The Social World of the Apostle Paul* (New Haven, Conn.: Yale University Press, 1983).

13. Norman K. Gottwald, *The Tribes of Yahweh: A Sociology of the Religion of Liberated Israel, 1250–1050 B.C.* (Maryknoll, N.Y.: Orbis Books, 1979).

14. Gottwald fully recognizes the formative role of the experiences of the "Moses group," but regards these experiences as preceding the history of Israel and as part of that history "only in the restricted sense that it was the experience of this Moses group, interpreted through its cult of Yahweh, which provided the basic, immediate historical catalyst, the communal forms, and probably a significant part of the repertory of cult symbols and practices for emerging Israel" (*The Tribes of Yahweh*, 38).

15. Walter Brueggemann, in his appreciative review of Gottwald's book, notes that the theologian will ask a range of questions that Gottwald does not address. See Walter Brueggemann, "The Tribes of Yahweh: An Essay Review," *Journal of the American Academy of Religion* 48 (1980), 441–51.

16. George V. Pixley, *God's Kingdom: A Guide for Biblical Study*, trans. Donald D. Walsh (Maryknoll, N.Y.: Orbis Books, 1981).

17. Gerd Theissen, *The Miracle Stories of the Early Christian Tradition*, trans. John Riches (Philadelphia: Fortress, 1983), 178.

18. See John Howard Yoder, *The Politics of Jesus* (Grand Rapids, Mich.: Eerdmans, 1972).

19. Robert W. Funk, *Parables and Presence: Forms of the New Testament Tradition* (Philadelphia: Fortress Press, 1982); John Dominic Crossan, *The Dark Interval: Towards a Theology of Story* (Niles, Ill.: Argus Communications, 1975); James Breech, *The Silence of Jesus: The Authentic Voice of the Historical Man* (Philadelphia: Fortress Press, 1983).

20. John Dominic Crossan, as in *The Dark Interval*, has been an eloquent representative of the total limitation of awareness to language. For a critique of this position, see John B. Cobb, Jr., "A Theology of Story: Crossan and Beardslee," in Richard L. Spencer, ed., *Orientation by Disorientation* (Pittsburgh: Pickwick, 1980), 151–64.

21. I have suggested earlier that "while most earlier encounters with this figure found an exclusiveness in Christ which insisted that Christ is the center of all meaning, Christ does not today impart the claim to be a universal logos that excludes all meaning which cannot be derived from it" (William A. Beardslee, *A House for Hope: A Study in Process and Biblical Thought* [Philadelphia: Westminster Press, 1972], 167).

22. Roger L. Shinn, "I Miss You, Margaret Mead," *Christianity and Crisis*, 38 (December 11, 1978), 304–06. Professor Shinn has commented at greater length on Margaret Mead in the March 4, 1985 issue of *Christianity and Crisis*.

23. Elisabeth Schüssler Fiorenza, *In Memory of Her: A Feminist Theological Reconstruction of Christian Origins* (New York: Crossroad, 1983), and *Bread, Not Stone: The Challenge of Feminist Biblical Interpretation* (Boston: Beacon Press, 1984).

24. *Bread, Not Stone*, xvi–xvii.

25. This assertion does not overlook the presence of a Christ image in our culture that is effective outside the bounds of the recognizable Church; see the discussion in John B. Cobb, Jr., *Christ in a Pluralistic Age* (Philadelphia: Westminster Press, 1975), chap. 1. But the specific traits of this image that derive from the New Testament will easily assume quite different functions while retaining the form given by their history. Thus the "Christ Figure" in literature may be put to ends that are unrelated to its original function; see Theodore Ziolkowski, *Fictional Transfigurations of Jesus* (Princeton, N.J.: Princeton University Press, 1972).

26. Gabriel Marcel, *The Mystery of Being* (Chicago: Henry Regnery, 1959), 153.

27. I have presented this view in more detail in *A House for Hope,* chap. 7.

28. See Martin J. Buss, "Self-Theory and Theology," *Journal of Religion*, 45 (1965), 46–53. The quotation in the text comes from a personal communication.

29. I have not been able to locate the reference for this quotation from Newman.

30. Will Herberg, ed., *The Writings of Martin Buber* (New York: Macmillan, 1958), 261.

31. In a slightly different form, this paper was presented as the Ernest Cadman Colwell Lecture at the School of Theology at Claremont, April 8, 1985.

5

POSTMODERN THEOLOGY AS LIBERATION THEOLOGY: A RESPONSE TO HARVEY COX

David Ray Griffin

A postmodern theology must be a liberation theology. One pervasive feature of modern theology has been a separation of systematic theology from theological ethics, especially social ethics. This separation has meant that systematic theology has articulated its doctrines of God, sin, and salvation with little or no reference to the concrete sins from which God is presumably trying to save us. Modern theology has thereby been abstract. This abstractness has made it appear irrelevant to the social evils of the time—the racism, the sexism, the social and economic injustice, the imperialism, the war, the nuclearism, the ecological destruction—which stand in contradiction to the will of God as portrayed in the theology. Discussion of these concrete social evils has been left to ethicists. Concern with overcoming these evils was thereby implied to be a secondary matter from a theological standpoint. All that one really needed to know about "the Christian faith" could be learned without getting involved in such matters.

This separation of theology and ethics is one illustration of the intellectual fragmentation characteristic of modernity. The modern university is organized into disciplines and subdisciplines, each with its own methodology, data, and theory. The modern seminary is likewise structured in terms of disciplines, under a general division between theoretical and practical fields. Although it is sometimes unclear whether ethics fits under the theoretical or the practical part of the curriculum, systematic theology is the theoretical discipline *par excellence*. Its methodology usually involves an alliance with some philosophical school of thought, at least some hermeneutical theory. Social ethics is usually aligned with some sociological school (which often means that it is not well informed by a systematic, philosophically grounded theology).

This separation of systematic theology from social ethics has had the effect of sanctioning the *status quo*. To speak of God, sin, and salvation without mentioning the concrete evil conditions of one's time and place is to imply that these conditions do not count as examples of the sin which God opposes. When the majority of German theologians in the 1930s and 1940s explicated the Christian faith with no negative reference to Nazism, they thereby implied that the politics of the Nazi party were not antithetical to the Christian faith. Ordinary German Christians, therefore, could be somewhat excused for not seeing that being a Christian at that time and place entailed opposing Nazism.

The chief point of liberation theologies, with regard to the nature of theology, is that this separation of doctrine and ethics, and hence of theology and sociology, must be overcome. Liberation theologians are thereby making a point that any authentically postmodern theology must incorporate. A postmodern theology must not simply seek to enunciate generally valid truths about reality—the nature of the world, of humanity, of God's saving purposes and *modus operandi*. These doctrines must be articulated in relation to the concrete issues of the theologian's time and place.

Postmodern theology as liberation theology must, therefore, always have two dimensions: the general and the particular, the universal and the local, the abstract and the concrete. Although some forms of liberation theology have, in reacting to the excessive abstractness of modern theology, virtually eliminated the universal dimension, postmodern theology needs to avoid replacing one type of one-sidedness with another. Without the universal, abstract element, the local, concrete analysis and imperative will be undermined. We cannot intelligibly say that "God wants *us* to work to liberate *these* people from *this* oppression" unless we can say that "God exists," that "God is for the liberation of the oppressed always and everywhere," and that "God does not effect this liberation unilaterally but only through the responsive co-operation of the creatures."

This is the perspective from which I approach Harvey Cox's presentation of postmodern theology as liberation theology in his *Religion and the Secular City: Toward a Postmodern Theology.*[1] In presenting postmodern theology as liberation theology, he stresses a point that some forms of thought called postmodern omit. His presentation thereby serves as a needed corrective. However, I will argue, the type of postmodern theology toward which Cox points is doubly inadequate. It is most obviously inadequate to the need for a postmodern theology to incorporate fully the modern concern with critical thinking aimed at articulating doctrines that are intended to be universally valid. But, more surprisingly, Cox's suggestions are equally weak with regard to the need for postmodern theology to be relevant to the particularities of the theologian's local situation.

The point of this critique is not to criticize Cox, but to use reflection on his proposal to grope toward a more adequate understanding of what a genuinely postmodern theology should be. All of us are victims of the modern mind-set, and our liberation from it will come only in steps, through an ongoing conversation. It is almost inevitable that the first attempts will be inadequate in many respects. I offer this critique in the spirit of a conversation with Cox, suggesting ways in which his own intuitions about what is needed could be carried out more adequately.

I. COX ON MODERN AND POSTMODERN THEOLOGY

For Cox, the most illuminating thing to say about modernity is that it is the world and worldview of the bourgeoisie, the capitalists. The function of modern religion has been to legitimate this world and worldview.[2] It has done this in part by accepting a divorce between religion and politics, so that religion is relegated to the inner life of individuals.[3] Modern theology has played its legitimating role by accepting this privatization of religion and by focusing on the skepticism of the educated class.[4] Modern theology by definition seeks to "interpret the Christian faith in relation to the 'modern' worldview."[5] Modern theology has taken as its main problem the doubts of the cultured despisers of religion, not the social problems of those who despise the modern world because they have been trampled by it.[6]

Whereas the modern age has been the age of the capitalists, Cox maintains, the postmodern age will be the age of the poor, the masses. Politics and religion will be reunited.[7] Theology will not be academic, but liberationist, meaning political from the outset.[8] It will not seek universality, but will focus on the particular concerns of the region,[9] knowing that unity comes not through agreement on ideas but through social conflict.[10] It will think in terms of the distinction between not believers and unbelievers but exploiters and exploited.[11] Theology will try not to revise popular religion to make it credible to elites, but to strengthen it as a resource for the oppressed.[12] Postmodern theology will be concerned less with the ideas them-

selves, and apologetic arguments for their truth, than with the social sources
and the political uses of ideas. [13] The sources for postmodern theology will
come not from the top and the center, but from the bottom and the edges. [14]
This means, concretely, that the sources will be popular piety and contact
with other religions. [15] Postmodern theology will thereby involve a fusion
of modern and premodern religious elements. [16] Postmodern theology, as
portrayed by Cox, will accordingly be drastically different from modern
theology.

II. POSTMODERN THEOLOGY AND TRUTH

One of the main questions to ask about postmodern theology is its relation
to truth. The reason for moving to a postmodern worldview, I would say,
is that the modern worldview is both untrue and unhealthy. Truth and pragmatism join in pulling us toward a postmodern worldview. In Cox's presentation, however, the argument seems to be wholly pragmatic. For example,
the modern worldview, as a cluster of ideas, is given little attention. The
concern with ideas as such is, in fact, dismissed as a modern preoccupation. There is no suggestion of the existence of a postmodern worldview
which is more consistent and adequate to all the facts than the modern
worldview. The concern with developing a coherent, systematic theology
is even ridiculed as a modern obsession. [17] Cox does raise the question of
truth at one place, [18] but his discussion there does little to counterbalance
his other statements and his performance.

One basis for advocating, in the name of truth, the shift from modern
to postmodern theology would be to argue that the latter reflects better the
nature and will of God. But Cox does not make this argument. He does
mention the problems of how we know that there is a God, and if so, that
this God is a God of the poor. [19] He recognizes that the problem of evil throws
into doubt the belief in a loving and all-powerful deity.[20] But he suggests
no answer beyond the purely pragmatic one of the liberation theologians,
that "one chooses the theory that works best, that helps poor people move
toward the goal of justice."[21]

Cox's justification for moving from modern to postmodern theology
is not philosophical or theological, but pragmatic and sociological. He suggests that modern theology was, for the most part, an admirable enterprise.
Modern theology was right to embrace modernity; it did a good job of tack-
ling the modern world; it provided, he says, a wide variety of plausible
answers to questions of modern intellectuals.[22] The reason for rejecting
modern theology is only that the audience and, hence, the questions have
changed. Fewer and fewer people, Cox maintains, are asking the questions
to which modern theology gave its answers.[23] In Cox's view, therefore, at
least according to some of his statements, there was nothing intrinsically
wrong with modern theology; he is moving beyond it only because its time
of useful service has passed.

One of the reasons Cox gives for the shift away from modern sensibilities which is occurring is that the previously accepted picture of the modern world has lost credibility. We are witnessing the collapse of the "five pillars of modernity"—confidence in science-based technology, the sovereignty of nation-states, bureaucratic rationalism, profit maximization, and the secularization and trivialization of religion.[24] Cox does not argue that these "pillars of modernity" were untrue, or based upon untrue ideas. His statement is the purely sociological one that they have "lost credibility."

Cox's purely pragmatic basis for moving from modern to postmodern theology means that his call is much weaker than it could be. His claim that we should move away from modern theology because fewer people are asking the questions to which it responds will leave unmoved the people who still find those questions important—which includes most of the people who will read Cox's book. Also, the shift from one audience (those interested in truth) to another (those interested in class conflict and justice) means that postmodern theology of this type will be no more inclusive than was modern theology: it will have simply shifted sides, while still serving only a portion of the human race. Finally, the refusal to call people to a postmodern theology in the name of greater truth leaves untapped one of the most powerful appeals. In particular, it misses the opportunity to connect the call to a liberationist theology with the widespread sense that the modern worldview has been profoundly limited.

An argument that the "pillars of modernity," which are a set of sociological practices and attitudes, were built on false foundations would require looking at some of the deeper assumptions of the modern worldview and at what the deeper assumptions of a postmodern worldview would be. To this deeper probe of the meaning of the contrast between modernity and postmodernity I now turn.

III. MODERNITY AND POSTMODERNITY

The sociological features of the modern world that are lifted up by Cox are rooted in ontological and epistemological doctrines. The basic epistemological doctrine is *sensate empiricism*, according to which knowledge of the world beyond ourselves comes exclusively through sense-perception. Given this assumption, there can be no knowledge of values. All moral and aesthetic values must be considered arbitrary preferences. Likewise, there can be no genuine religious experience, in the sense of a direct experience of God. Belief in God is therefore entirely groundless, or at best rooted in an inference from our sensory knowledge of the world.

The basic ontological doctrine of modernity is the *mechanistic doctrine of nature*, according to which the physical world is composed of inanimate, insentient atoms which interact by deterministic impact. This mechanistic view of nature allows for two possible worldviews, which are the two worldviews of the modern period. In the dualistic version, the human self or soul is regarded as above nature, and as the only locus of value in the world. Dualistic modernism therefore leads to alienation, anthropocentrism, and intellectual fragmentation in the form of a radical split between the sciences and the humanities. This dualism is unintelligible apart from supernaturalism, because a supernatural deity is needed to explain the interaction of sentient mind and insentient matter.

Because of the difficulties inherent in it, dualistic modernity has increasingly collapsed into modern materialism, which entails determinism, reductionism, atheism, and nihilism. When combined with the sensate empiricism which it implies, this worldview entails positivism, the view that the only truth we can know is that which comes through the natural sciences. Religion, theology, ethics, and metaphysics can deliver no additional truths, according to this perspective: we can reasonably believe only the worldview that is provided by the natural sciences and that is a worldview in which there is no God, no freedom, and no meaning to the distinction between good and evil.

This worldview fosters the type of modern world described by Cox. The atomistic mechanistic view of nature, in which relations are based on force alone, promotes an atomistic, mechanistic view of society, ruled by bureaucratic rationality. At the international level, this view promotes a system of power politics between nation-states. This worldview also promotes a technology devoted to perfecting instruments of coercion and death and an economic system in which profit is the only standard of excellence. Finally, this worldview relegates religion to illusion; of course, it can be an illusion that is useful (from the modern perspective), insofar as it promotes nationalism, militarism, and economically efficient behavior, and/or provides enough solace to individuals to keep them keeping on. But it is still an illusion.

The sociological features of the modern world are, therefore, based upon modern philosophical assumptions. To say this is not to argue for the absolute psychological or temporal priority of the philosophical to the sociological. We, indeed, have good reason to believe that some of the modern philosophical beliefs were in part sociologically motivated. My argument is only that the sociological attitudes and practices have been supported by the philosophical foundations. Even if a strong case could be made for the complete priority of the sociological, it would still be true that the philosophical beliefs have been used to justify them. Accordingly, to the extent that the philosophical foundations of modernity can be shown to be false, the sociological attitudes and practices and institutions built upon them can be shown to be inappropriate. To show the superiority of postmodern philosophical beliefs would be to show the greater appropriateness of a postmodern world.

This philosophical dimension is, however, entirely missing from Cox's analysis of modernity and postmodernity. He does at one place ask what is common to "modernism" in theology, philosophy, literature, the arts, economics, and political science.[25] But he answers this question in terms of the "five pillars" mentioned earlier, thereby taking the sociological categories of economics and political science as normative. The meanings of modernism that are foremost in philosophy, religion, literature, and the arts, some of which I summarized above, are simply ignored.

This lacuna in Cox's diagnosis makes it superficial, which means that his remedy is also superficial. By ignoring the interconnection between the philosophical and the sociological aspects of modernity, he fails to show the depth and the extent of the changes that are needed if we are to move into a genuinely postmodern world.

The absence of the philosophical dimension is also relevant to the failure, noted earlier, to provide any but a purely pragmatic justification for moving beyond modern theology. Cox's assertion that modern theology provided plausible answers to the questions directed to it must be shocking to anyone conversant with the problems of modern theology. Insofar as modern theologians sought, as Cox rightly says, to "interpret the Christian faith in relation to the 'modern' world view," that is, in terms of an acceptance of that worldview, they had taken on an impossible task. Within the context of the modern worldview, theologians could give few plausible answers to the central questions, such as: How can the world be understood as God's creation? How can we know there is a God? How can we be free and therefore responsible? How can we speak of immortality or resurrection? How can our lives have any ultimate meaning? Why should we treat each other as ends, not simply as means? How can any theological assertions be thought to be true? Whereas Cox praises the way modern theology "tackled the modern world,"[26] the truth is that modern theology let the modern world tackle *it*. A postmodern theology that sees this, and that sees that the philosophical assumptions of modernity are open to philosophical challenge, need not justify the movement from modern to postmodern theology on a pragmatic basis alone. It can also justify it in the name of truth.

Parts of Cox's own discussion point to the need for this type of philosophical analysis. For example, he refers to August Comte's positivism, according to which "the exclusive way to truth lay through scientific experiment," and then adds that Comte therefore "could not believe in the miracles and the absurdities of religion."[27] But Comtean positivism rules out not only those things that are normally connoted by the terms *miracles* and *absurdities* but also *God, freedom, values,* and any form of *immortality*—precisely those beliefs taken by Kant and many others to be the basic presuppositions of religion. Without a critique of modern positivism, we cannot distinguish viable religious beliefs from absurdities.

This question of the credibility of "miracles and absurdities" is not a trivial one for Cox's program. He says that "a careful appreciation of popular piety must constitute the heart of a postmodern Christian theology."[28] But it is precisely those things classified as "miracles and absurdities" by the modern mind that are at the heart of popular piety. Indeed, Cox makes his statement in the context of a discussion of the shrine of Our Lady of Guadalupe, the story of which involves an appearance of the Virgin Mary and a miraculous imprinting of a picture. Cox speaks of a "careful" appreciation of such things. By what criterion is an appreciation "careful"? Do we accept the modern worldview and therefore "appreciate" such stories while demythologizing them? Or do we appreciate such stories in terms of a postmodern worldview that allows for the occurrence of types of events that had been ruled out as absurdities by modernity? Again, Cox says that the "postmodern enterprise requires a conscious and critical reappropriation of selected elements of the premodern," adding that modern theology could not carry out this reappropriation because it was based on a repudiation of all those features of popular religion that made it "an anomaly in the modern world."[29] But to speak of a "critical" reappropriation of "selected" elements implies a critical standard of judgment. Such a standard requires an ontology and epistemology which tell us what is possible and impossible. Most of the anomalous elements of popular piety, which have been rejected by modernity as "miracles and absurdities," involved nonsensory perception, or some other form of action at a distance, or both. We can have a "critical" reappropriation of such elements only if we have a postmodern ontology and epistemology that allow for such events.

Without a critique of the philosophical assumptions of modernity, the "critical reappropriation" of elements of premodern religion will probably be simply one more example of modern demythologization. For example, Cox says that the central proclamation of postmodern Christian faith will be the resurrection of Christ and the human body.[30] But what does Cox *mean* by resurrection? He nowhere rebuts the modern view, which is that, in his words, no one "needs a specialist on heaven and the soul when neither one exists."[31] And his most precise definition of resurrection seems to be: "God alive in the world, life defeating death."[32] This affirmation is clearly important, and it goes far beyond what the modern worldview would allow (unless this affirmation is in turn to be demythologized). But it does *not* affirm what popular Christian piety means by resurrection. The belief in resurrection that has emboldened Christians to stand up to national security states, whether that of Rome centuries ago or those of our century, is not only that God is alive, but also that God will preserve *our* lives beyond the form of existence they have in these mortal bodies. Through this belief, Christians (and others) have held that, although their bodies were subject to the state's coercive power, their ultimate identities were not. Unless postmodern theology can reaffirm belief in resurrection in *this* sense, no real reappropriation is taking place.

One more problem arising from the failure to analyze modernity in terms of its ultimate philosophical and theological assumptions is the virtual equation of modernity with capitalism. This virtual equation hides the fact that most socialist visions and governments have been equally modern. Indeed, Karl Marx was more fully modern than was Adam Smith, being (at least in his later period) more scientistic, more deterministic, and more materialistic, as well as more atheistic. It is debatable whether or not Marxist socialism has been less individualistic; but, in any case, it has limited its sense of social community to the human species, being as fully anthropocentric and therefore as ecologically destructive as capitalistic ideologies. A more adequate analysis of modernity will help us see that a postmodern theology, and a postmodern world, must go beyond modern socialism as well as modern capitalism.

Cox's apparent ambivalence on the importance of critical thought concerned with the truth of ideas is related to an ambiguity on the meaning of *postmodern theology* and therefore its anticipated authors. On the one hand, following a suggestion by Pablo Richard, Cox predicts that postmodern theology will be developed by those who never became fully modern—who were excluded from, even trampled by, the modern world, or for some other reason did not fully absorb it.[33] This side of his thought explains his attention to Third World thinkers and his otherwise inexplicable attention to fundamentalists.[34] On the other hand, he suggests that postmodern theology will be developed only by those who have passed through the modern world—who became fully modern, then realized modernity's weaknesses as well as its strengths.[35] It is this side of Cox's thought that is reflected in the book's title and its concluding sentence: "No one can move beyond the secular city who has not first passed through it."[36] When he is in this mood, Cox stresses the importance of critical thought: to be postmodern is to retain the critical spirit of modernity in the face of the recent return of the sacred.[37]

This latter side of Cox's thought is the viable one: no one can be postmodern without having absorbed the values of modernity, and careful, critical thought is one of its chief values. There is some truth in the other side of his thought; this truth is that postmodern thinkers can and should learn from people who have not fully absorbed modernity. But one cannot expect those who have never become modern to articulate a *post*modern theology.

For Cox to carry through consistently the viable side of his thought would overcome a related ambiguity regarding the meaning of *modern theology*. Cox characteristically suggests that a theology is modern by the mere fact of "addressing itself to the modern world of ideas," or to "the 'modern' world view."[38] But surely a theology that *addresses* the modern worldview in order to reject it should not be called *modern*. A modern theology is one that *accepts*, for the most part, the modern worldview. Cox shows recognition of this point by adding that modern liberal theology, which did in the main accept the modern worldview, is the "most characteristic expression" of modern theology.[39] Carrying out this point consistently would enable Cox to define postmodern theology as one that deals critically with, and thereby transcends, the worldview upon which modern theology was based. He would thereby avoid suggesting that to become postmodern is to give up modernity's critical spirit and its concern for the truth of ideas.

IV. THEOLOGY AND PARTICULARITY

Cox's adumbration of a postmodern theological stance is deficient not only with regard to theology's task of seeking truths valid for all Christians, indeed all human beings, but also with regard to the dimension of particularity, or local concreteness, required by a liberation theology. This weakness is exemplified in three ways.

In the first place, although Cox is a (North) American theologian writing primarily for an American audience, he advocates a style of theology that is appropriate, if at all, only in other locations. I refer here to his rejection of the treatment of ideas themselves and the defense of their truth (apologetics). I refer in particular to his quick dismissal of basic questions such as the existence of God and the challenge of the problem of evil to the notion that God is on the side of the poor, and to his belittling of the concern for a "coherent and systematically unified" theology which seeks universally valid truths. The rejection of these concerns reflects the situation in countries in which the modern worldview and the Enlightenment critique of religion have not permeated the culture deeply, and in which the truth of Christian faith can be largely presupposed. As Cox himself points out, "historically, liberation theology in Latin America has arisen on a continent where critical thought has focused more on the misuse of Christianity than on skepticism."[40] But the situation is quite different in the United States, where the modern worldview with its critique of religion is widely dispersed and has even permeated the churches. In *this* context, not to address the question of the truth of religious ideas is not to address one of the real concerns of people.

Whereas liberation theologians of various sorts have rightly accused modern theology of a false universalism, in which a theology written by white, middle-class males in North Atlantic countries was assumed to be the norm for all people,[41] we must also avoid a reverse form of false universalism. A postmodern theology, especially one written for Americans, must deal with the question of truth and justified belief. And, because in a post-authoritarian age the claim to truth can only be made in terms of consistency and adequacy to the facts of experience, postmodern theology must be *more*, not less, coherent and systematic than modern thought. To say this is not to deny the importance of Cox's concern for a style, perhaps that of narrative, that does not "drain the color from religious expressions."[42] But it is to deny that narrative and colorful expressions can obviate the need for careful, systematic thought aimed at showing the harmony between our best religious and ethical intuitions and our best scientific and philosophical thinking.

A second form of the lack of particularity in Cox's proposal is the absence of any reference to the role of his own country, the United States, in the global system of economic, political, and cultural oppression from which most Third World liberation theologians are seeking liberation. These Third World theologians certainly know of the role of the United States, and they write profusely about it. But they are not in position to do much about it. It is American Christians who are in position to do something significant to change U. S. foreign policy. But this cannot occur until more than a tiny fraction of the American Christians understand the American role in the global network of poverty, injustice, militarism, and terrorism. This educational task is not going to be carried out by the government-supported public schools, nor by the mainline media, which are, for the most part, controlled by individuals and corporations who benefit from current American policy.

It would seem that the first task of an American-based liberation theology is to carry out this educational task. Cox does refer to capitalism and of the need "to address the systemic forces that determine how people live," but the references are abstract.[43] He also says: "Eventually we North Americans will have to develop our own liberation theology."[44] But the term "eventually" suggests that it is less urgent for there to be liberation theology here than in Third World countries, whereas the dominant role of the United States in the global system of oppression makes it *more* urgent. Finally, Cox gives no hint as to the concrete issues with which an American liberation theology would deal. The liberationist dimension of an American postmodern theology will have to be very concrete about the changes needed in our own country if we are to bring its policies into harmony with the activities of our Liberating Creator and with the possibility of a postmodern global civilization.

A third example of the lack of particularity in Cox's proposal for a postmodern liberation theology is manifested by his failure to stress the philosophical-theological side of modernity (discussed above in section III). Whereas one precondition for a widespread liberationist movement among American Christians would be a widespread knowledge of actual American policies, as mentioned in the previous paragraph, a second precondition would be for American Christians to have a firmly held religious view of the universe that freed them from nationalistic idolatry, materialistic greed, and the inclination to use military means to protect American privileges in the world (for example, 6 percent of the world's population using between 30–40 percent of its physical goods). They would have such a view if they firmly held that God is the supreme power of the universe; that divine power is the power of evocative, persuasive love, not the power of coercive, violent destruction; that the persuasive power of nonviolent love will eventually overcome evil with good; that soul and its qualities are more real and more power-ful than what we call matter and its qualities; and that our ultimate identi-ty, meaning, and salvation cannot be secured through material abundance or threatened by the loss thereof. But most American Christians, having to a considerable extent internalized the modern worldview, do not have such a view. Conservative and fundamentalist theologies present some features of such a view, but only some and not persuasively, because they do not show how this view is compatible with the world as known through science. Modern liberal theologies do not even present such a view because it is in-compatible with the modern worldview. A postmodern liberal theology, if it is to be liberating in our context, must effectively convey such a view.[45]

SUMMARY AND CONCLUSION

Harvey Cox's proposal for a postmodern theology contains many things that should be affirmed, and it is good to have his important voice saying them. Like Cornel West's, Cox's form of postmodernity does not relinquish the liberationist project of modernity, but reaffirms and expands it. His pro-posal overcomes the modern divorce between theology and ethics. He sees that the liberationist motive is rooted in religion, and that popular piety, often condemned by liberationists, can be a great resource for social, political, economic, and cultural liberation. He stresses the need to fuse the best of modernity with selected elements from premodern religious life which had been too quickly dismissed by moderns. And he sees the need to over-come the arrogance of the false universalism of North Atlantic theology.

At the same time, Cox's proposal needs to be improved in two major aspects. On the one hand, the truth of basic assumptions of the modern worldview needs to be challenged in the name of more adequate, postmodern assumptions. Accordingly, modern theology should be defined not as a form of theology that *dealt* with the modern worldview but as the form of theology that *accepted* it. On the other hand, theologians in the United States, which is a superpower and which inculcates a high proportion of its population with the modern worldview, should not discuss liberation theology as if the forms it takes in Third World countries would be ap-propriate here. We must develop a form of postmodern theology that refers concretely to the sources of oppression in our own country and that will have liberating effects in the American churches and for American public policy.

NOTES

1. Harvey Cox, *Religion in the Secular City: Toward a Postmodern Theology* (New York: Simon & Schuster, 1984).

2. *Ibid.*, 82, 198, 202.

3. *Ibid.*, 20, 55, 58, 183, 184, 200, 242.

4. *Ibid.*, 164, 212.

5. *Ibid.*, 177, cf. 183, 166.

6. *Ibid.*, 179.

7. *Ibid.*, 20, 127.

8. *Ibid.*, 234.

9. *Ibid.*, 178, 212–13.

10. *Ibid.*, 157.

11. *Ibid.*, 159.

12. *Ibid.*, 164, 212, 242.

13. *Ibid.*, 155, 266.

14. *Ibid.*, 21, 175–76.

15. *Ibid.*, 96, 150, 216, 240, 244.

16. *Ibid.*, 240, 258.

17. *Ibid.*, 213.

18. *Ibid.*, 225–28.

19. *Ibid.*, 151.

20. *Ibid.*, 146–47.

21. *Ibid.*, 152.

22. *Ibid.*, 21, 159, 161–62, 177.

23. *Ibid.*, 159, 177.

24. *Ibid.*, 183–90.

25. *Ibid.*, 182–83.

26. *Ibid.*, 21.

27. *Ibid.*, 206.

28. *Ibid.*, 244.

29. *Ibid.*, 241.

30. *Ibid.*, 209, 214, 215, 254.

31. *Ibid.*, 199.

32. *Ibid.*, 263.

33. *Ibid.*, 201–02, 208.

34. *Ibid.*, 50, 72, 97, 267.

35. *Ibid.*, 268.

36. *Ibid.*, 268.

37. *Ibid.*, 20, 171, 258.

38. *Ibid.*, 266, 177, cf. 164, 183, 212.

39. *Ibid.*, 268.

40. *Ibid.*, 155.

41. *Ibid.*, 178, 212–13.

42. *Ibid.*, 213.

43. *Ibid.*, 82, 125, 134, 190.

44. *Ibid.*, 267.

45. I have presented a first statement of such a view in *God and Religion in the Postmodern World* (Albany: State University of New York Press, 1989).

6

THE CULTURAL VISION OF POPE JOHN PAUL II: TOWARD A CONSERVATIVE/LIBERAL POSTMODERN DIALOGUE

Joe Holland

The term *postmodern* in Christian theology, as this volume illustrates, embraces various visions. I have been intimately involved with two of these postmodern visions. One, a liberal postmodernism, arises out of modern sources and is well represented in this series. The other, a conservative postmodernism, arises out of premodern sources and is probably less well known to readers of this series.[1]

I explore here one of the foremost thinkers of this conservative postmodern theology, Pope John Paul II. I use this exploration as the occasion to propose a creative dialogue between conservative and liberal postmodernism. Such a dialogue may belong to the essence of postmodernism.[2]

This essay is divided into three sections. Section I provides an interpretive framework for locating the distinction between the liberal and conservative postmodern visions. Section II examines the postmodernism of John Paul II, which I regard as the deepest and broadest voice in the conservative postmodern stream. Section III proposes some issues for dialogue between the conservative postmodern vision of the Pope and the liberal version of American postmodernism.

Before proceeding to the body of the essay, however, I would like to share some of my own story, to explain how I was led to see the postmodern exploration as needing a dialogue between liberal and conservative intellectuals.

Over the past twenty years, my approach to theory and practice has been heavily influenced by modern liberal culture, which led me initially to explore postmodernism from the liberal side. This influence came especially from pro-Enlightenment social thinkers such as Hegel, Marx, Durkheim, Weber, and from the modern political practice of democratic socialism and movements for community organizing, civil rights, peace, Third World solidarity, labor, feminism, and ecology.

During the last ten years, however, I watched fresh intellectual and political energy coming from conservative sources—part of it disturbing, but other parts intriguing. At the same time, I watched many liberals lose touch with popular culture while conservatives pursued a deliberately populist strategy. I tried to study carefully this new conservative strategy, both its New Right and neoconservative variants.

This experience led me to remember an earlier stage of my intellectual development when I studied the great classical thinkers of the Western cultural tradition, made available to me through the Catholic theological heritage. In this remembering, I began to understand better the conservative critique of the Enlightenment, especially of its drive toward psychological autonomy uprooted from the historical-structural mediation of tradition and community, of its loss of symbolic ground leading to the privatization of religious energy, and of the nonrenewing hypermasculine character of the entire process of mechanistic modernization.

In this study of the conservative strategy, I noted that, while certain conservative thinkers sought a classical cultural restoration to shore up the threatened legitimation of advanced capitalism, more profound conservative thinkers offered a consistent critique of modernity, including capitalism. This more profound conservative critique, wishing to preserve the institutional mediation of past tradition and bonded community, focused in a classical manner on the structural theme of subordination of the self to authority and the historical theme of conservation of the past (in contrast to the modern focus on freedom of the self from authority and on progress toward the future by release from the past). This more profound critique seemed open to dialogue about fresh postmodern possibilities.

One might say that this more profound conservative vision can be open to the future, provided the institutional mediation of tradition and community would not be dissolved by modern disintegration. So I became aware that the liberal-conservative debate was not simply between the excesses of modernization, on the one hand, and the recapture of forgotten classical roots, on the other.

Out of this exploration, I perceived that a new postmodern cultural form was being born, although that form was not fully clear. Many of my liberal friends were already probing this postmodern notion, and I learned much from them. But I also felt that the liberal exploration of the postmodern vision carried residual assumptions from the destructive side of modernity. Many of these liberal postmodern pioneers were profoundly uprooted from their own tradition and community. Such future-oriented individualism gave them the freedom to explore the fresh cultural vision before others. But it also meant that they perceived the new vision through the lenses of modernity's strategic weaknesses. It meant that they might be seeing only part of the postmodern vision.

It was then that I judged that other parts of the postmodern vision might be better seen by a conservative exploration. I was delighted to find a thinker who provided for me seminal confirmation of this hypothesis, namely Simone Weil, especially her pioneering ''postmodern'' (she does not use the word) book, *The Need For Roots*.[3]

Later I found a Catholic conservative postmodern school increasingly centered in the thought and writing of Pope John Paul II. While I am not aware that the Pope himself explicitly uses the term *postmodern*, I found constant references in his writing to the crisis of modern culture and to the birth of a new cultural form. The Pope wrote constantly of the exhaustion of modern ideologies and of the birth of a new global consciousness of human solidarity.[4] Confirming this impression, *New York Times* correspondent E. J. Dionne, Jr., has cited Rocco Buttiglione, an Italian philosopher known to be close to the Pope, as saying,

> . . . the Pope is not 'premodern', as many of his critics portray him, but 'postmodern'. He doesn't attack Marxism or secularism because he thinks they're the wave of the future. . . . He sees their time as already having passed. He's looking beyond them, to the future.[5]

In a similar vein, the neoconservative Lutheran theologian Richard John Neuhaus, in his book *The Catholic Moment: The Paradox of the Church in the Postmodern World*, has sketched John Paul II as a leading conservative postmodern thinker and ecclesial strategist.[6] I agree with Neuhaus that the Pope's vision is postmodern, but I do not ultimately agree with his interpretation of the Pope's vision. Neuhaus wishes to use John Paul's thought against socialism and in defense of capitalism. But as John Paul's recent encyclical *Sollicitudo Rei Socialis* (*Social Concern*) makes undebatably clear, the Pope is profoundly critical of both modern socialism and modern capitalism as socially mechanistic, geopolitically imperialist, and ecologically destructive.[7] I believe that Neuhaus's current thought, despite its thoughtfulness, needs ultimately to be classified as a late modern ideology using classical Catholic themes to defend the threatened legitimacy of modern capitalism. By contrast, John Paul II increasingly distances himself from both liberal and collectivist modern ideologies. He returns to drink from the Catholic tradition, but he is also willing to explore a new cultural expression of global human solidarity which reaches beyond capitalism and Marxism.

Out of this reflection, I made the judgment that the two sides—conservative and liberal explorations of the crisis of modern culture—carry complementary strengths and weaknesses. I concluded, therefore, that dialogue between conservative and liberal strands of postmodernism is necessary to avoid deepening the ecological, social, and spiritual fissures created by modernity. More important, I came to see this dialogue as an indispensable condition to birthing a fully postmodern culture.

I. THE INTERPRETIVE FRAMEWORK[8]

In setting a framework for discussing John Paul II's thought, I first propose a theory of the journey of human culture, then locate the liberal and conservative postmodern visions in terms of the heritage of this journey.

Four Stages of Human Culture

In many places, I have sketched an ideal typology of four broad stages or types of human culture and described them as primal, classical, modern, and postmodern. My typology, tracking the journey of Western culture, is rooted in forms of the political economy, religious institutions, means of communication, and underlying sexual symbolism of the Divine. It is based on my own adaptation of insights from Thomas Berry, Marshall McLuhan, and Erich Neumann, originally triggered by Gibson Winter's work on root metaphors.[9]

This ideal typology is only a heuristic device. It fails to do justice to the rich heritage of human culture. But I have found it helpful for locating various tendencies in the late modern and early postmodern cultural debate.

The four stages of this sketch are both sequential and cumulative. It has been the tendency of liberalism to liberate the future from the past and of conservatism to protect the past against the future. But I believe the postmodern perspective will see past and future as organically mutual, with the past being the roots of nourishment for the future's expanding branches. When I speak of different stages of communication and spirituality, therefore, the new stages do not replace prior ones.

In this four-stage sketch, I attempt to classify distinct forms of spiritual energy. I do this not from the viewpoint of Christian theology but in terms of the underlying natural spiritual energy of the cultural community. According to Catholic theology, which has understood grace and nature to be complementary, and indeed all creation analogously to communicate its divine source, such an exploration of natural spirituality is a precondition to a formally Christian (in my case Catholic) spirituality.[10]

In these stages, I refer to sexual metaphors in symbolic terms. These feminine and masculine symbols are not taken rigidly to define actual women or men—the experiential correlative of these symbols is found in a range of male and female experience. But neither are they taken to be entirely disassociated from the real sexual identity of women and men. I suggest that the real psychic and social experiences that correspond to the feminine symbol are found more in women's experience, and that the real psychic and social experiences that correspond to the masculine symbol are found more in the experiences of men. I am thus taking a middle position between the conservative tendency to rigid sexual definition and the liberal tendency to treat sexual differentiation as psychically and socially irrelevant. In my view, sexual differences are fundamental but not absolute.

I. The Primal Stage: This stage refers to the preclassical (even preneolithic) roots of the human journey, where human consciousness had a mystical-holistic sense of unmediated communion with the natural environment, its particular social community, and the Creator whose presence it saw as transparent in all creation.[11] Berry refers to it as the *tribal-shamanic* stage. As McLuhan would tell us, its only means of communication was *speech.* Neumann sees it as the time of the original creation myth—when the religious image of the *great earth mother* was dominant, with the male symbol not fully differentiated from it. In this stage, human consciousness perceives itself within the webs and cycles of nature.[12]

In this stage emerge what we might call the *feminine technologies.* During this period, women seem to have invented speech, agriculture, domestication of animals, weaving, homebuilding, pottery, the use of natural medicines, and many other foundational technologies of the bonding and cycles of human community.[13]

I describe the spirituality of this stage as the *spirituality of immanence.* The sacred is revealed in the mystical communion across time and space for all creation. The sacred is experienced simply by entering fully into the maternal womb of the cosmos. The incarnational, sacramental, and liturgical dimensions of Christianity are in part grounded on this primal spiritual vision. In biblical terms, the Garden of Eden symbolizes this original blessing, the Covenant with Noah its precarious survival, and the Kingdom of God its redemptive and eschatological retrieval in a healing and deepening way.

In sum, the primal stage is a tribal-shamanic form, grounded in the communication of speech, enhancing human society by female technologies of unification, and nourished by a spirituality of immanence centered in the feminine-cosmic symbol of the great earth mother.

2. *The Classical Stage:* Early in humanity's journey occurs a dramatic break with primal innocence. Many cultural traditions record this rupture. The Christian tradition refers to it as original sin. As the Book of Genesis tells the story, the event precipitates an ecological, social, and spiritual alienation. But the rupture also awakens humanity's God-like technological creativity, which can then be used, in Moses' words, to choose life or death.

The alienation externalizes itself in a growing spiral of technological masculine violence—from Cain, to his great-grandson Lamech, to Lamech's son Tubal Cain. While Cain's name may mean "metal worker" (suggesting an early use of metal tools and weapons), Tubal Cain was a forger of vessels of copper and iron (suggesting the Bronze age with more mature metal tools and weapons). The violence goes from Cain's sevenfold vengeance to Lamech's *seventy times* sevenfold vengeance.

It is here that male technologies emerge, based on the experience of separation, in contrast to the female technologies, which were based on unification. These masculine, breaking technologies of separation led over a long history to the emergence of the great classical empires made possible by metal tools, including weapons. These empires were based on the extraction by elites, living in fortified stone cities, of an economic surplus from large agricultural populations served by massive irrigation systems controlled from the stone cities.

One of the major uses for this surplus was the building of stone monuments: phallic-like towers, pyramids, and temples. Defining the spiritual meaning of this system, and especially the rhythm and structure of its agriculture, was a new kind of religious elite: priests who separated the sacred from the profane, the religious from the secular. They replaced the creation-oriented shaman who lived within the community and saw the sacred in everything. By contrast, the priests stood above the people to appease the Divine, now seen as above creation, and to mediate Its message to the people below. Following Berry's initial pattern of analysis, we can describe this stage as *hierarchical-priestly.*

McLuhan would tell us that one of the foundational technologies making possible the growth of these empires was the invention of *handwriting,* used by imperial elites for religious texts, trade and production records, and political laws and treaties. Out of this technology and its imperial context emerge the great world religions of a holy book.

From the handwriting of this stage comes the Torah of Judaism and the Bible of Christianity. Yet the religion of Israel was born not from Egyptian imperial power but from God's liberation of its oppressed. Similarly, Christianity was born not at the center of Roman imperial power but from its periphery in Palestine, and even there at the margin of Galilee.

Neumann sees the emergence of this stage in terms of the myth of the hero. It was the search of the masculine principle for its own identity outside the maternal womb and not modeled on the feminine pattern. He notes that, in the creation myth, the womb was the symbol not only of birthing but also of devouring. The great mother brought forth life and crushed it afterwards, meaning that the male symbol was constantly sacrificed to the female symbol. The emancipation of the hero and his arduous and violent journey in search of identity is the birth of the male principle.

In the classical stage, the masculine symbol was thereby identified with the transcendence of nature's cycles. That masculine search had both a spiritual and a scientific-technological character, legitimated by the divine image of the sky father. By contrast, the feminine symbol was now divided into a higher image of wisdom *(Sophia, Sciencia)* beyond nature, and a lower image of the webs and cycles of nature. Sexuality, linked to the webs and cycles of nature, was identified with the lower side of the feminine symbol, and the male was identified with flight from the temptations of the lower sexual woman to search for the higher spiritual woman. The masculine way of religious transcendence became the higher way; the feminine way of natural immanence became the lower way. The feminine symbol was divided into material and spiritual poles, and the masculine symbol was identified as a journey from the material pole to the spiritual one.

In classical Christianity, the higher masculine way of transcendence belonged to monasticism, the lower (sexual) feminine way of nature's webs and cycles to the laity. For this reason, few laity were canonized as saints—unless they were virgins, widows, or martyrs.

The spirituality of this stage was the spirituality of *transcendence*, the attempt to find the holy above the webs and cycles of nature. For the Jewish and Christian stories, it was here that patriarchal transcendent religion of the heavens did battle with matrifocal immanent religion of earth—the *sky father* against the earth mother. Here, too, we find the origin of warrior images of the divine. But it is also here that the spiritual and technological struggle against the sacrifice of human life to nature begins. In the biblical story, Abraham is both the first Jewish patriarch and the one who turns from the human sacrifice of his own son.

In the initial journey side of the biblical story, beginning with events such as the call of Abraham and Moses and expressed especially in the tribal confederation of Shechem, this transcendence takes on a prophetic-historical character: the religious journey into history as a way of growing beyond the limits of nature's repetitive cycles. Here God transcends nature through historical intervention. The Protestant Reformation stressed this historical dimension of the biblical vision.

But the other dimension is its priestly-spatial character, symbolized by the fulfillment of the journey in the land of promise and particularly in its urban temple—the city of David on Zion and later the temple of Solomon. Here the journey fades and the special celebration of the cosmos predominates. But the cosmos is no longer the womb of the sacred earth mother; it has become instead the kingdom over which the sacred warrior king and sky father presides—from an outside and transcendent point. Catholicism stressed this spatial dimension of the biblical vision.

Paradoxically the assertion of divine transcendence separating the holy from nature, whether in time or space, can be viewed as a new stage of humanity's conscious relationship to nature. By stripping nature of its primal spiritual numinosity, the spirituality of transcendence made possible a masculine historical-technological relationship with nature. The great temples and monasteries were places where the seeds of modern science and technology were planted. [14]

In sum, the classical stage is a hierarchical-priestly form, grounded in the communication of handwriting, enhancing yet also threatening society by male technologies of separation, and nourished by a spirituality of transcendence centered in the symbol of the sky father.

But it is important to remember that this patriarchal cultural form, although it rose to dominance in world history, nonetheless often functioned as a veneer resting fragilely upon the still strong primal undercurrent of matrifocal culture. The classical stage was thus the storm at the top of the sea, while deep down much remained unchanged from the primal era. Thus, the classical distinction between high culture and popular culture. This residual power of the primal feminine technologies would only be fundamentally threatened in the modern cultural stage.

3. *The Modern Stage:* The birth of modern culture, centered in the North Atlantic nations, was midwifed by the communications revolution of mass *printing*, first in craft form and later in industrial form. Printing made possible the expansion of the vernacular, which led to the modern nation-state as well as to the expansion of education and specialization, which in turn promoted the growth of modern science and technology. The final form of all this development was modern industrial societies of mass democracy committed to the liberal principles of freedom and progress. Accompanied by a new form of spirituality, which I discuss in a moment, the print communication technology led to a social form which we might describe as *industrial-pietistic.*

Even before the print revolution, when the dynamism of modern science and technology was breaking beyond the monastic womb, a new social institution came to the fore—the university. Similarly within Catholicism, as the new commerical cities laid the groundwork for the modern economy, so the Benedictine monastic order went into decline and a new mobile urban-based form of the religious order took its place, namely the mendicants, particularly the Dominicans and the Franciscans. These orders were intimately tied to the new universities. Umberto Eco's novel, *The Name of the Rose*, is a masterful study of this cultural shift. [15]

But even this revolution in the form of the religious order would not be sufficient to contain the new energies, once the print technology (originally a Chinese invention) was harnessed in the West. As a result, a new form of Christianity was born—Protestantism—based on the vernacular and the printed Bible distributed to the popular culture. Following the birth of this new form of Christianity and of the Catholic response to it, dramatic long-term changes occurred in the cultural life of the West.

First, the classical commitment to transcendence was despiritualized and historicized. Masculine transcendence over the cyclically feminine dimension of nature became separated from spirituality. The male principle was no longer expressed as male religious asceticism questing for feminine yet unworldly spiritual wisdom *(sophia)*. Instead, *sciencia* grew into modern science, with its totally masculine technological attempt within history to triumph over feminine nature. [16] The classically masculine principle of transcendence was carried into modernity while being uprooted from its originally religious form (a development which deepened the liberation in early classical civilizations of the noble class from the priestly class). Transcendence formally shifted from a vertical to a horizontal plane—from asceticism to history. And in the process it lost completely its feminine goal of *sophia* or *shalom*.

Second, spirituality was returned to the feminine symbol, but in a way different from the primal form. Just as transcendence was historicized, so spirituality was psychologized (and eventually privatized). Spirituality became the soft feminine realm of subjective inner feelings, mediated by family and other forms of primary community but disconnected from the hard masculine realm of objective outer technologies. Spirituality returned to the symbol of the feminine womb, but the womb was no longer the symbol of the cosmos. Rather, the womb of spirituality became a private place within the psychological recesses of the self, or at most of primary groups. This can be called the spirituality of *interiority*.

One explanation of why this split occurred is offered by Thomas Berry in his essay, "The New Story." [17] According to Berry, the Bubonic plagues which began in the fourteenth century fundamentally disrupted Western cultural consciousness. Berry estimates that in Constantinople, for example, the plague killed between one-third and one-half of the entire population in twenty years. This social trauma led to two distinct cultural responses: psychological-spiritual retreat from creation and technological-scientific attack on it.

The first response uprooted the Christian doctrine of redemption from its matrix in the doctrine of creation. This approach severed religion from the outer world, stressing instead the inner psychological experience of the Savior and the inner psychological experience of faith, especially in terms of subjective feelings. This was the symbolically feminine side of passive aggression toward creation. The second response laid the foundation for a secularized drive toward modern science and technology, with its own scientific priesthood, intent on gaining control over nature by empirical manipulative techniques—to prevent such catastrophes in the future. This was the symbolically masculine side of active aggression toward creation. Though one was formally religious and the other formally secular, both might be seen as drives for redemption. (Berry does not develop the sexual-symbolic side of this split, at least not in this essay. That is my addition.) Returning now to my own reflection, we can note that the Protestant Reformation, with its rejection of the visible mediation of the tradition and community through the formal institutional authority of the church, and with its elevation to primacy of the principle of individual conscience, gave powerful expression to this spirituality of interiority. But it was also found in the Catholic *devotio moderna* of Thomas á Kempis, the psychological exercises of Ignatius Loyola (to be done in a psychological manner alone), and the devotional practices of modern apostolic religious orders. Indeed the Catholic retreat house, a modern creation, became the central Catholic place of this spirituality of interiority. Devotionalism became the popular Catholic form of this spirituality of interiority, spiritual direction its elite form.

That this modern spirituality, both Catholic and Protestant, should be described as predominantly feminine in character may seem to contradict the feminist critique of the Church as a patriarchal institution. That critique is true if one looks at the institution in political terms, that is, in terms of its formal authority structure, which is so obviously masculine. But if one looks at the Church as a cultural structure, it is clear that its energy is predominantly feminine. Any number of studies have shown that the vast majority of active participants in the inner life of modern Western churches are women, while activist men give priority to commitments in the outer technological world. [18]

This split between the masculine and feminine symbols into the polarization of objectivity/subjectivity, technology/psychology, outer/inner, and secular/religious, while taking various forms, became the deepest symbolic division of modernity. C. P. Snow described it as the division of two cultures. [19] Robert Bellah and his colleagues have described it as the split between the instrumental individualism of corporate life, with its managerial ethos, and the expressive individualism of private life (including religion), with its therapeutic ethos. [20]

The split's most dramatic expression was the zoning segregation between work and family, which followed the Industrial Revolution. As industrial society developed, Christian churches were built almost exclusively on the "feminine" residential (consumer) side, not on the "masculine" technological (producer) side. As developing networks of industrial transportation widened the space between work and home, religion became more privatized and life more fragmented.

In this split, the primal dominance of the earth mother and the classical dominance of the sky father both yielded to what I call the sibling rivalry of feminine spirituality and masculine technology. Masculine technology seemed intent upon rendering itself autonomous from feminine spirituality, while feminine spirituality seemed intent upon becoming private, isolated from masculine technology. Increasingly, religion became the feminine realm and society the masculine realm, with sibling battles between the two.

The healing of this split in recent decades is more apparent than real. Although in late modernity women have increased their participation in the outer technological world, they have been strongly pressured to do so in masculine ways. Similarly, although many men have turned to religion in the crisis of modern society, they frequently look to it as a soft place of rest and refuge from the harshness of the outer society. As a result, even though the social and religious worlds may be less segregated in gender terms, in symbolic terms the split has been deepening.

In distinction from the classical experience, where high classical culture functioned as a veneer upon the still powerful primal culture, modern culture began to disintegrate its classical and primal roots. This happened as male technologies, intensified by the industrial revolution, began to expand their power dramatically and to absorb into the industrial revolution the formerly female technologies.

A dramatic, if threatening, achievement of modern culture was effectively to separate large masses of the population from the land into urban centers of human fabrication—something which had been possible in times past only for small elite percentages of the population and even then in extremely limited ways.

Equally dramatic was the weakening of the family system. The family, once the center of religion, economic production, and human nurture, was increasingly treated as an incompetent unit—to be stripped of its religious, productive, and nurturing functions and converted into a place of consumption in refuge from society.[21] This process may have begun when the Counter Reformation strategy of Catholicism, to prevent Protestantism from spreading across Catholic territorial boundaries through the kinship system, attempted to uproot Catholic evangelization from its ancient root in the kinship system. It substituted instead a new bureaucratic model of parish and apostolic religious orders whose members were separated in cult-like fashion from their biological families.[22] The apostolic orders, displacing the mendicants, created in effect a Catholic department of health, education, and welfare, which then fed into the creation of the modern welfare state. Throughout this development, the family began to appear as a consumer of social and church services, rather than creator of society and church.

The weakening of family intensified with the invention of television, one of the early steps in the electronic revolution. Television began to obliterate modernity's separation between the hard values of the outer, masculine, technological world and the soft values of the inner, feminine, familial world. Now the main instrument of socialization was no longer the former feminine combination of family, religion, and school, but television—planted in the middle of the home and displacing the traditional hearth. The private/public balance was no longer viable.

In summary, the modern stage of human culture is the industrial-pietistic form, grounded in the communication technology of print, maximizing the male technologies with industrial power and even taking over in masculine manner the female technologies, and symbolically nourished by a retreating spirituality of interiority which is psychologically feminine in character and stands in competition with the encroaching masculine technological exteriority of the outer social world.

4. *The Postmodern Stage:* The ensuing ecological, social, and spiritual crisis of the modern split leads, I believe, to the newly birthing stage of postmodern culture. Because this stage is just now being born, offering a mature statement of its life is difficult. But, based on the pattern of the above analysis, I offer some projections of it as an ideal type.

First, the *electronic* communication technology midwifes the birth of the postmodern stage and grounds its development. This technology has dramatically expanded its power with the microelectronic revolution. The integrated circuit, the silicon chip, the computer, the communications satellite, television, electronic mail—these are all phenomena that will fundamentally reshape our culture and our spirituality. Speech, handwriting, and print, on the communications side, and immanence, transcendence, and interiority, on the spirituality side, are not displaced, but they are all reorganized under the leadership of the new form.

Second, the scale of social organization weakens the dominance of the modern nation-state and moves toward a global/local symbiosis. Electronic communication and transportation simultaneously make the planet a single economy (and, therefore, a single society), and a decentralized one rooted primarily in local institutions open to global interaction. Satellite communications, combined with jet transport, already have made the economy global. The miniature scale of the new technology will make it also local.

Third, an important dimension of this miniaturization of the technology will be, I propose, the rerooting of the economy in the family. The Industrial Revolution uprooted the economy from family life only because the technology became physically so large and economically so expensive that it could no longer fit in the household or be purchased by household finances. (We take the industrial separation of family and work as normal, yet in the human journey such separation is but a historically shallow and geographically limited event.) The new electronic technology is not only small but increasingly inexpensive, making it accessible again to a household base. Presumably in the future the family will recapture from large bureaucracies not only large dimensions of the social functions of health, education, and welfare, but also production itself. Technological planners who have produced the incredible phenomenon of desktop publishing are already speaking of desktop manufacturing.

Fourth, because the new technology is simultaneously expanding and integrating all information, we are already seeing a new synthesis of natural, social, and spiritual information in the context of a holistic yet dynamic ecology of life. Human society in its global/local character is increasingly perceived as integrated, with that integration in turn extending to our natural environment and to the spiritual source from which it flows. (A central dimension of this integration will be the search for technological forms that blend with and enhance the webs and cycles of our natural and social environments, rather than the modern pattern of technological interventions which flatten the cycles and shatter the webs.) The metaphor of ecology, both holistic and dynamic, becomes the metaphor of all of creation, including its religious and social dimensions.

Fifth, the spirituality of this society is increasingly the spirituality of *cocreativity*. We humans become aware that we are the consciousness of planet earth and to some degree the consciousness of the universe. The function of our consciousness is to deepen the creative communion of the life process, including its natural, social, and spiritual dimensions. We become aware of our solidarity as a human family, and discover that, unless we create new forms of human solidarity, we could well destroy life on the planet. We become aware that our solidarity extends to the entire ecosystem of the planet and beyond to the universe—with equally great possibilities of death or life. We become aware finally that our solidarity extends to the Creator of life, from whom our own creativity proceeds and with whom it joins in profound communion, and that the ecological-social choices of technological patterns are ultimately choices of death-dealing idolatry of a false god or life-giving worship of the Creator.

The postmodern technological patterns, flowing from the above principles, might be described as a new synthesis of the heritage of female and male technologies, now seen as reciprocal and mutually enhancing, indeed maturely creative in their embrace. Following the earlier pattern, we might describe this electronic, global/local, family-centered, holistic/dynamic society as *ecological-mystical* in character.

In this new context, I propose, our fundamental spiritual symbols—the primal earth mother of immanence, the classical sky father of transcendence, and the modern sibling rivalries of feminine psychological interiority and masculine technological exteriority—will be retrieved and yet converge in a fresh model of fertile sexual embrace: the *creative communion* of the female and male symbols as our analogical image of the fertility of society, nature, and Divinity. In Catholic terms, the sacrament of marriage becomes the postmodern image of the Divine, of nature, and of society, which is in turn rooted in the creative communion of the Trinity.

According to my proposal, then, the postmodern stage is an ecological-mystical social form, grounded in the communications technology of electronics, integrating for the first time in a balanced yet creative way the female and male technologies, and nourished by a spirituality of ecological-social-Divine cocreativity symbolized by fertile sexual communion.

The following chart gives a summary of these four stages in terms of the social/religious form, the innovative means of communication, the innovative spirituality, and the dominant sexual symbol system.

CHART II
The Stages of Human Culture

Stage	Form	Communi-cation	Spirituality	Sexual Symbol
Primal	tribal/shamanic	speech	immanence	earth mother
Classical	hierarchical/ priestly	writing	transcendence	sky father
Modern	industrial/pietistic	print	interiority	sibling rivalry
Postmodern	ecological/ mystical	electronics	creativity	fertile embrace

The Conservative and Liberal Explorations

Against the horizon of this analysis, we can now look at the conservative and liberal explorations of postmodern culture. In the profoundly modern split between science and religion, liberal postmodernism arises primarily from the modern scientific tradition, while conservative postmodernism arises primarily from the modern religious tradition. Both agree that modern culture is breaking down and that a new cultural form is being born. But they disagree on the nature of that new cultural form and how we should midwife its birth.

1. Liberal Postmodernism: The first postmodern school explored here, which I label liberal, emerges primarily from within modernity's secular trajectory, and finds in its unfolding logic a postmodern breakthrough.[23] In the microelectronic era, with a technological explosion of information and its connections, the scientific consciousness begins the journey to a new stage. Its initial impetus lies with new developments in scientific consciousness, especially new insights from physics, ecology, and developmental psychology, and a holistic scientific paradigm made possible by the microelectronic revolution.

A religious form of liberal postmodernism has also emerged, but it draws on liberal theological sources, which leaned toward the secular/scientific side of modernity. Religious postmodernists in the liberal school tend to be critical of existing Christian institutions as traditionalist and authoritarian. They often appeal to resources outside the dominant strands of the Christian tradition or to hidden or recessive dimensions of the Christian tradition itself. These past resources are either carriers of the primal tradition (such as preneolithic cultures, Native Americans, Celtic mystics) or sexually more balanced versions of classical spirituality (from the East rather than from the West).[24]

Liberal postmodernists, whether of secular or religious origin, usually remain committed to core dimensions of the modern liberal vision—an orientation more to future possibilities than to actual past tradition, and to an individualistic uprootedness from traditional mediating institutions. The future takes priority over the past (except the primal past) and the individual takes priority over institutional mediation (even though community—now voluntaristically understood as the connecting of individual choices—becomes a central theme). Liberal postmodernism nonetheless seeks to ground the new ecological scientific insights in a mystical vision. It thereby represents the scientific side of the modern split reaching toward the spiritual.

We might, in sum, describe the religious form of liberal postmodernism as growing initially out of scientific sources, at least partially alienated from traditional religious institutional mediation of the Christian West, searching for a more ancient wisdom in primal roots, and seeking to update the religious consciousness with the gifts of the postmodern scientific breakthrough.

In terms of the preceding ideal-type analysis of four stages of human culture, the liberal exploration of postmodernism grows out of modern secular culture, seeks a mystical-ecological ground for postmodern science, and looks for inspiration back to the feminine symbol of immanence in our human origins of the primal stage. The liberal exploration thus draws on the primal and modern to reach for the postmodern. But it tends to reject the classical stage, with its still strong heritage of spiritual transcendence and institutional mediation, and above all it tends to reject the emergence there of the masculine symbol.

A major part of my own formation has been in this liberal stream, so I am deeply in its debt. But I carry two fears for the liberal exploration in isolation from the conservative exploration. First, I fear that, by rejecting the masculine/classical stage, liberal postmodernism, in fact, breaks the communion of the dynamic whole, and thus threatens to miss the holism which it so profoundly seeks. Its one-sided and uprooted search for holism could be stillborn. Second, I fear that, by concentrating exclusively on the feminine symbol, it threatens to reinforce the late modern violence which is based on the outer-directed flight of the masculine symbol from the feminine symbol and on the inner-directed feminine flight from the masculine symbol. The phallic side alone becomes a sword, while the womb side alone becomes a tomb. Only the embrace of the two taps into the full genetic and cultural heritage of our ecological history. Only the embrace of the two continues and deepens the spiral of regeneration.

2. Conservative Postmodernism: The other postmodern school explored here, which I label *conservative*, grows out of classical resistance, most often religious, to modernity. Its roots are to be found in the aristocratic critique that accompanied modernity's own birth and development, for example, the Romantic movement and its historical links to Catholicism. Conservative postmodernists see the classical critique of modernity being vindicated by the modern breakdown and the postmodern breakthrough. Tending toward a cyclical rather than linear view of history, they are naturally drawn toward a return to classical roots. In turn, they are appalled by the appeal to primal roots, which they see as pagan and maternally threatening to devour the fragile masculine achievements of human civilization.

But if the conservative consciousness only looks for a return to classical forms, it cannot be classified as *post*modern. Only if it is truly open to new possibilities, along with the continuity of tradition and the authority of structure, does it warrant the name *postmodern*. These new possibilities need to be more than simply a new classical-modern synthesis, as is proposed by late modern neoconservatives. The new possibilities must, instead, embrace something beyond both the classical and modern imaginations—for example, John Paul II's imaging of a new global human solidarity and his ecological concern for the fate of the earth.

This conservative postmodern school grows more formally out of religious sources, and so tends to draw less on new developments in scientific consciousness. It tends, in fact, to address late modern technological life in ethical rather than mystical terms. Just as the liberal exploration of postmodernism hungers for spiritual depth but tends to resent and bypass the actual religious traditions of the West, so the conservative exploration of postmodernism hungers for a science infused with wisdom but tends to resent and scold the new mystical consciousness actually emerging within postmodern science. The scientific side finds it difficult to come to terms with its religious parallel and vice versa. The scientific side fails to recognize its origins in classical religion, and the classically rooted religious side fails to see the new mystical energy rooted in postmodern science. The sibling rivalry continues.

In terms of the preceding four-stage ideal typology, the conservative exploration of postmodernism rejects the primal stage and the secular side of the modern stage, seeking to ground the postmodern possibilities primarily in the legacy of the classical stage. By so doing, it tends to see the masculine symbol as carrying the active side of creation and the feminine symbol as largely passive or receptive. That perception was, of course, originally based on a mistaken biological model that shaped the classical philosophical images of transcendence and immanence. In that model, the female was seen as providing only a nest for the male seed, which was seen as carrying the fullness of life. We know today that life comes only from the mutual activity of the male and female principles. The religiously symbolic consequences of that shift are enormous. Even so, I am grateful to those on the conservative side who have preserved the importance of our classical heritage. In my early formation, I learned much from it and hope that future generations will have this opportunity. But I also have fears about the conservative side in isolation from the liberal side.

First, I fear that its exclusive identification of spirituality with the masculine principle of transcendence (important as transcendence remains) impoverishes the religious imagination and denies it the feminine gift of immanence. I see immanence as the necessary complement to transcendence for the two to fuse into the spirituality of cocreativity.

Second, I fear the religious reassertion of the male principle alone. It does perform the important function of challenging the retreating or passive-aggressive flight of the feminine spirituality of interiority from masculine technological exteriority. But if that challenge leads to the displacement of the feminine, rather than to embrace with it, then the male religious principle will only legitimate the growing monopoly of the male technologies, whose outwardly destructive principles now threaten the entire ecosystem. It will also drive the feminine symbol deeper into recessive interiority, so that society will be denied its birthing power.

3. Toward a Creative Synthesis: Obviously, according to this analysis, the need is to break beyond the polarization of the feminine and masculine symbols in spirituality and science and to find a cultural path to fertile embrace. This means accepting both symbols and their full unfolding of our primal, classical, and modern heritages; avoiding the legacy of deformations from each stage; rerooting the masculine symbol in the cycles of regeneration and welcoming the feminine symbol into linear history; expanding the recessive feminine technologies of unification and linking them with a diminished scale for the masculine technologies of separation; and unfolding the mutually creative feminine and masculine dimensions of ecology, society, and Divinity.

II. THE CULTURAL VISION OF JOHN PAUL II

Against the horizon of the preceding ideal-type analysis, we can now look at the cultural vision of Pope John Paul II. The following analysis is drawn from an essay I wrote on the Pope's teachings on the role of the laity in society.[25] Despite the focus on the Catholic laity, the reader should be able to grasp John Paul's wider cultural vision.

I will set as a context for the Pope's teaching his claim that modern culture is in crisis and that a fresh postmodern, yet past-rooted, culture is struggling to be born. Then I will interpret his teaching on the laity's social role as a strategic ecclesial response to the crisis of modern culture. Finally, I will briefly suggest some areas of dialogue between John Paul and liberal American postmodernism, particularly on the Divine, ecological, and human meaning of the sexual symbols.

John Paul II's Cultural Analysis

John Paul asserts that modern culture is in crisis.[26] In his view, because politics follows culture, and because modern culture is in crisis, the primary task is not to struggle politically within the modern framework but to seek transformation at the cultural root.

The Pope's critical analysis of modern culture is the key to his profound and urgent focus on the role of the laity in society. From this analysis flows an ecclesial strategy centered on four social themes: (1) culture, (2) laity, (3) family, and (4) work. For John Paul, culture is the strategic terrain, laity the strategic carrier, and family and work the strategic areas of the lay challenge. This entire framework is then set in a spiritual framework of transcendence and creativity, partly premodern and partly postmodern.[27]

1. Existential Roots: John Paul's critique of modern culture is deeply existential. His experience of modern life has been filled with personal and social suffering.[28]

The social suffering was staggering. In his formative years, he lived under the Nazi occupation. His graduate studies, his strong interest in theatre, and his poetry all had to be conducted clandestinely. Around him death was common. Even the end of the Nazi occupation of Poland only marked the beginning of Soviet domination. He could not help but note that both the Nazis and the Soviets were entirely modern, mobilizing the most powerful technological resources of their time.

This experience was compounded by deep personal suffering. His mother died when he was nine, his brother while he was in high school, and his father when he was twenty-one. In addition, in two serious accidents he was nearly killed. The attempted assassination upon him as Pope was one more hurt in a long list of personal pain.

According to Joaquin Navarro, a Spanish psychiatrist and the Pope's chief spokesperson, John Paul's spiritual outlook cannot be separated from this bitter suffering.[29] Having passed through a profound personal cross and through the social cross of modernity's destructiveness, he plunged (with a heroic rejection of despair) into a mystical search for personal strength and social renewal. Out of this search grew his critique of modernity as a culture of death and his attempt to formulate a postmodern life-centered spirituality of transcendent cocreativity.

2. The Crisis of Modern Culture: According to John Paul, modern culture is revealing itself as a mechanistic civilization of Faustian destruction, fundamentally threatening human dignity and ultimately human life.[30] The main expression of this degradation is the instrumentalization of humanity by its own modern technological tools. This technological instrumentalization of humanity is seen as flowing from modernity's loss of spiritual transcendence, leading to a loss of human transcendence (called *secularization*) and of human creativity.

Obvious structural signs of this modern instrumentalization are communism's *political* oppression of the Second World (the communist nations) and capitalism's *economic* oppression of the Third World (Africa, Asia, and Latin America).[31] But apparently more fundamental, for his view, is the *cultural* seduction of the First World, perhaps especially in the United States, because America is the propagandizing center of modern culture and thereby the crucial key to the entire modern project.[32]

In other words, for John Paul, modernity's economic and political oppression is derivative from its cultural seduction. In the case of the Second and Third Worlds, oppression comes politically or economically from outside the heart of the social experience (for example, through the foreign corporation or the uprooted state). But in the First World it comes from within—through the seduction of the inner self and its cultural imagination.

John Paul describes this seduction of the self as the ideology of consumerism.[33] By this he means not simply that the affluent sector of the First World consumes too much, but more profoundly that the First World is losing the spiritual transcendence of its own creativity. Consequently, in his view, the First World fabricates a shallow, plastic, even destructive culture of manipulative instrumentalization, whose artifacts it then hedonistically worships.

If cultural seduction is the key to political and economic oppression, a key to cultural seduction, according to John Paul, lies in the experience of sexuality.[34] He sees the consumer ideology beginning in the deepest recesses of the self, convincing the self that sexuality is no longer a bipolar fertility-creating community in which the family transmits life to future generations. He sees sexuality having become for modernity, at worst, a trivial instrument for instantaneous gratification or, at best, a source of personal fulfillment (both detached from familial bonding across time and space).

In John Paul's view, the attack on sexuality quickly becomes an attack on the regeneration of human life. A contraceptive culture emerges, human conception is uprooted from marriage and becomes the manipulated object of technological control, and abortion turns into the rallying cry for liberal female liberation. For this culture, with sexuality uprooted from familial fertility and reduced instead to a valueless manipulation, family and its outgrowth in community erode.

For this reason, he evidently fears the liberal vision of the liberation of women,[35] which appears to promote the liberation of woman from family and procreation. The liberal vision of female liberation is seen as destroying the feminine symbol and as collapsing society into the sterility of an aggressive but nonregenerative mechanism grounded solely on the masculine symbol. The modern struggle over the symbol of woman is thus seen as the struggle between humanity's death and life. Defense of the creative mysticism of the female symbol becomes for John Paul defense of life itself.[36] Denying the fertile renewal of life through human sexuality, First World modernity finds, according to this view, an easy path to the economic degradation of labor and to the political abandonment of the poor, and correlatively to the expansion of militarism. In this perspective, if the inner psychic creativity of the sexual self can first be so instrumentalized and rendered infertile, then the outer technological creativity of the community of labor can easily be degraded and pointed toward destruction.

3. *An Apocalyptic Spirituality:* Arising directly from John Paul's cultural analysis is his apocalyptic spirituality, at once highlighting the crescendo-like power of historical evil and announcing the joyful healing of Jesus' cross. For John Paul, the cultural crisis is at root a spiritual crisis.[37] The struggle is not simply with a misguided technology, but with death-dealing forces of evil taking on a demonic character. Linking this theme of the demonic to the symbol of the fertile woman, he powerfully alludes to the Book of Revelation's passage about the dragon pursuing the woman and seeking to devour her child.[38] The apocalyptic dimension is further heightened by his strong references to the impending Third Millennium, as if it marks an ultimate moment of human history.[39]

Overcoming such deep pessimism is John Paul's belief in the power of the Cross to regenerate personal and social life amidst the modern personal and social death. Suddenly the pessimistic analysis yields to optimistic proclamation. The modern civilization of death can be healed by the new life of the Gospel. Christians as a new humanity can help to create a new civilization of love.

John Paul places great hope in the personal and social power of conversion. For his view, regrounding the civilization in recognition of divine transcendence at the personal and social levels is the strategic spiritual response to the crisis of modernity. For him, the construction of a postmodern civilization flows first from an act of faith.[40]

Following the recovery of transcendence, in this view, the task of cultural reconstruction entails linking the scientific skills of modernity with the traditional spiritual wisdom of the classical European Christian past. John Paul is not suggesting that society can return to a classical European model. But he is proposing a creative encounter between the future-oriented modern scientific project and the tradition-rooted heritage of classical European Christianity—as the precondition of creating a postmodern civilization.

John Paul's first step in restoring past wisdom is to recall the classical European interpretation of the first chapters of the Book of Genesis.[42] There he finds the proper order of life according to the classical Western model of transcendence. In contrast to modern civilization, where he sees the material world triumphing over humanity to its destruction, he finds in Genesis the opposite model, in which humanity is called to master and to dominate over the material world. For him, it is now the task of transcendent spirituality to reaffirm humanity's call to mastery over nature, to prevent modernity's perversion of this order from destroying humanity.

The sexual symbols also come into play for John Paul. In the Jewish and Christian scriptures, for the most part, the masculine symbol appears to image the Divine, the feminine symbol to image the human. Humanity is seen as feminine opening itself to penetration by the masculine character of divine transcendence. Only then can humanity share in the creativity of divine transcendence, wherein it is called to transcend nature by mastering it. Whereas in relation to Divinity the human represents the feminine symbol, in relation to nature it represents the masculine symbol. Within the human, woman is then seen as embodying the feminine symbol of receptivity, while man is seen as embodying the masculine symbol of activity. This whole perspective recalls the classical *spirituality of transcendence*, which was a spirituality centered in the masculine symbol.

Certain cultural strains in late modernity have rebelled against this masculine hierarchy of the sexual symbols. In John Paul's perspective, however, the aggressive style of this rebellion reveals the collapse of the feminine into the masculine. He sees late modernity liberating women by eliminating what has traditionally been called the feminine function in society. Late modernity's aggressive attempt to liberate women from a cultural posture of receptive dependence and from the biological role of life-bearer is further taken as symbolic of the whole modern rebellion against the Creator. The material world is seen as now dominating humanity because modern humanity as a whole attempts to reject its feminine dependence on the Creator. According to this view, humanity, seeking to gain autonomous control of life, paradoxically loses the authentic source of its creativity and collapses into an evil project of death. Healing this project of death entails, for John Paul, a spiritual restoration of the feminine dependence for all humanity, male and female, on the symbolically masculine transcendent Creator.

The Strategic Role of the Laity

I turn now to what this cultural analysis and spiritual response mean to the Pope for the laity. To do this, it is necessary to explore two foundational spiritual principles in his teaching on the role of the laity in society: first, the distinct social role of the laity concerning transcendence, in contrast to the role of clergy and religious; second, the lay realization of spiritual cocreativity in family and work.

1. Transcendence: For transformation of the modern crisis, John Paul looks strategically to the laity, whom he sees as called to permeate society with the leaven of the Gospel. This will happen, according to his teaching, by the laity's assisting society to recognize divine transcendence and to embody that recognition in personal habits and social structures. This recognition will then ground the derivative recognition of human transcendence over nature.[43]

For this teaching, the clergy and religious are to be public witnesses before society to the eschatological dimension of the principle of transcendence. By contrast, the laity are to be public witnesses to the transformative power of the principle of transcendence in the social order. In other words, from the cultural viewpoint, the clergy and religious are primarily a sign of the absolute nature of transcendence (perceived by John Paul in eschatological rather than cosmic terms), and, therefore, live at some psychological and sociological distance from normal human endeavors. They are not called to work out the practical implications of that sign for social structures, for then they would lose their eschatological significance.

According to this view, the laity are called to work out the implications of transcendence, to make recognition of transcendence permeate the institutions of society. They are not called to stand outside society, for then it would be impossible for them to make transcendence transformative. They are to embody recognition of transcendence within the temporal order or, in more evangelical terms, to be the salt of the earth, the light of the world, the leaven in the mass.

In this teaching, the primary institutional sphere of action for the clergy and religious is the church, wherein they influence the laity. By contrast, the primary institutional sphere of the laity is not the church, but the society. To understand better this eschatological/transformative division of labor, it may be helpful to delve into its conceptual roots.

In classical thought, as we saw before, reality was conceived as a hierarchical (meaning the "rule of the holy") chain of being descending from the higher spiritual realm to the lower material realm.[43] Classical European Christianity appropriated this concept as foundational for its interpretation of reality, calling the higher, eternal realm *religious* and the lower, temporal realm *secular*. For classical European Christianity, this led to two ways or distinct states of life among Jesus's disciples: (1) the "perfect state" of monasticism (and derivatively other forms of "religious" life and by extension clerical life), and (2) the implicitly "imperfect state" of the laity. Again, various terms—*temporal, material, secular,* and *lay*—were used to describe this imperfect state.

The key to the distinction between the two states was the cyclical concept of time. Time's cycles of degeneration and regeneration were seen as lower (meaning *material*) than the higher (meaning *spiritual*) way of eternal, universal, absolute truth. The meaning of this key is further revealed when we discover that the word *secular* has its root in the Latin word for *sexuality* (*secus*). The lower world, because it is sexual (that is, subject to death and in need of biological regeneration), is not seen as transcendentally spiritual. As mentioned earlier, these two states were given a sexually symbolic character. The higher spiritual dimension was portrayed in terms of the male symbol, perceived as transcending the cycles of nature. The lower material realm was portrayed in terms of the female symbol, perceived as representing the immanent cycles of nature.

Drawing on this classical, hierarchical distinction between the male and female symbols, which was Christianized by classical European culture, John Paul's teaching on the laity seems implicitly (and occasionally explicitly) to propose a complex set of symbolically male/female interactions, interpreted according to the classical European model of transcendence.

First, as mentioned earlier, humanity is seen as symbolically feminine in its call to be submissive before the transcendent mastery of a symbolically masculine God. This pattern is repeated when the church is interpreted as the bride of Christ (as much earlier in the symbolic husband/wife relationship between Yahweh and Israel). Yet humanity is seen as symbolically masculine in its divine-like vocation transcendentally to dominate the symbolically feminine realm of nature.

Second, lay Christians take on distinct symbolic sexual roles in the ecclesial and social spheres. In the ecclesial sphere, where they are part of the spiritual order, they function as receptively feminine. In the social sphere, where they are part of the temporal order and called to dominate nature, they take on a transcendent masculine character.

Third, there now appears within the temporal order yet another symbolically male/female division between the roles of the laity in the world. The masculine character applies to the lay experience of work (meaning the transformation of nature or work outside the home). The implication is that this sphere is more proper for men, although that theme is muted in John Paul's teaching. By contrast, in the familial or biological sphere of the life cycles the lay role is again feminine: to bear life and nurture its cycles. The implication is that the home sphere is more proper for women, although a family role for men is increasingly emphasized.

Adapting the dualist distinction of classical European culture to the modern context, we might say that John Paul sees modern culture's interpretation of both the masculine and feminine symbols as pathologically disfunctional at the foundational religious, human, and natural levels.

First, for this view, the symbolically feminine receptivity of humanity to the Divine is seen as transformed by modernity into the symbolically masculine quest after science as mechanistic manipulation. In this modern view, technique displaces wisdom and the masculine symbol seeks only itself. According to this interpretation, modern society's technological, masculine stress on autonomy needs to be healed by accepting its own symbolically feminine receptivity before divine transcendence. This acceptance will then enable human work to assume its proper transcendent posture of masculine mastery over feminine nature.

Second, for this view, the symbolically feminine function of sustaining and renewing the material cycles is seen as spurned by modern society. Modernity is interpreted as repressing biological regeneration by contraception and abortion, uprooting women from family life, and defining their role in terms of masculine mechanistic values of modern civilization. Modern society's female side, accordingly, needs to be healed by preventing the feminine symbol from being mechanistically collapsed into the masculine symbol, by protecting the classically female renewal of the human life cycles (especially by opposing contraception and abortion), and by honoring the family and the classical role of woman in the home.

For John Paul, each of these two tasks—first, the reorientation of science toward spiritual transcendence and of work toward human transcendence (healing the male symbol) and, second, the biological renewal of the human life cycles (healing the female symbol)—takes programmatic expression in the two strategic structures, namely work and family. Here there comes into play the second principle of John Paul's lay spirituality, namely cocreativity.

2. *Cocreation:* Work and family are two key themes of John Paul's teaching on the role of laity in society. On work, he has written the most radical document of the modern Catholic social tradition, *Laborem Exercens* (1981). On family, he has written an equally radical document, *Familiaris Consortio* (1981). These two documents constitute the foundation of his institutional approach to the role of the laity in society.

Each of these documents carries what John Paul considers a foundational social principle. For *Laborem Exercens*, it is the explicit principle (in the realm of history) of the priority of labor over capital. For *Familiaris Consortio*, it is the implicit principle (in the realm of nature) of the priority of family over the individual.

Grounding both these principles is the Pope's principle of humanity's vocation to be cocreator with the Creator. Through work and family, in this view, humanity becomes, with God, cocreator of its own species and of its material production. This cocreativity, seen as rooted in the symbolically masculine transcendence of the humans over the rest of creation and flowing from the symbolically masculine transcendence of the Divine over the human, is at the heart of John Paul's lay spirituality. His approach to lay spirituality thereby links the principle of premodern transcendence with the postmodern principle of cocreation.

But each of these expressions of human cocreativity with the Creator is linked with a distinct sexual symbol. The sphere of work, meaning the historical transformation of nature, is viewed in symbolically masculine, transcendent terms, analogous to the rule of God over creation. The sphere of family, meaning the cyclical renewal of human life across the generations of time and across the kinship of space, is viewed in symbolically feminine, receptive and generative terms, revealing the role of humanity as creature open to God's creativity.

Based on John Paul's teaching in *Laborem Exercens*, the social mission of the laity for the sphere of work would be to restore the foundational social principle of the priority and solidarity of labor. At the root of John Paul's social analysis is the idea that modern industrial civilization has taken on a mechanistic character. Capital (meaning humanity's technological projects) has been treated as the master of labor (meaning especially the working class, but also management). While there is a class structure to the social domination of capital over labor, the deeper pathology is the treatment of all labor as the instrument of technological production. This treatment denies that labor is the source of the creativity of work, instead portraying technology as the source and labor as its tool. John Paul calls this the inversion of the principle of the priority and solidarity of labor.

This inversion, according to John Paul, began under capitalism. Capitalism treated labor as "merchandise" (a synonym for Marx's *commodity*) to be bought and sold according to supply and demand, with no inherent rights. Labor thus became the object of production rather than its subject, its tool rather than its master. Many rightly rebelled against this degradation of labor.

But the alternative that appeared, namely industrial socialism, failed to restore the priority of labor. Focusing on political mobilization of the working class, the modern socialist movement sought to give control over production to labor. Instead, it only shifted the domination from capital to a totalizing state, with labor still its instrument.

The reason for this failure, according to the Pope, is that the modern socialist movement moved only at the surface level of politics, failing to challenge the foundational culture of modernity. It failed, he says, to address the loss of Divine transcendence at the heart of the modern pathology, and thereby failed to rediscover the human transcendence that flows from it. The real struggle is over meaning, not force.

For John Paul, both modern ideologies—capitalism and socialism— are losing energy. From this cultural point of view, modernity is wearing out and failing to renew itself. A foundational task for the laity is to restructure the work process so that it is grounded on the dignity of the person, in turn flowing into the priority and solidarity of labor.

Restructuring the work process according to the priority and solidarity of labor is seen to imply many things. It means exploring a cooperative economics, perhaps marked by worker ownership, a share by labor in management, and profit-sharing. It also means recognizing that the person is more than a cog in the machine and bears economic rights—for example, the right to employment, a just wage, health care, rest, a pension and insurance, a safe environment, and the right to form unions. The state, the "indirect employer," has a real responsibility for the common good and needs to promote economic planning. In addition, the scale of the work question is no longer simply one of classes within a nation, but is now truly global.

Finally, the structure of work should not undermine the family. It should pay the head of the family a family wage so that the wife will not need to work outside the home. In this way, John Paul proposes, mothers can fulfill their primary mission to the children. Yet even where women work outside the home, he says (following the model of classical transcendence), it should be in accordance with their nature (the receptive feminine symbol). The advancement of women should be structured in such a way that they do not have to abandon what is specific to them—at their own expense and at that of family. Because there is no reflection in *Laborem Exercens* on the role of fathers with children, mothers appear (in this document) to have the unilateral responsibility for children.

Turning now to *Familiaris Consortio*, John Paul says that the social mission of the laity for the familial sphere is to restore the priority and solidarity of the family. Modern society is increasingly misfounded on a vision of autonomous individualism, rooted in a quest for autonomous self-affirmation, which is a corruption of the idea and experience of freedom. The result of this atomization is that life is increasingly extinguished or prevented from beginning, and the loving bonds of community erode.

But, John Paul insists, the individual is not the starting point for society. Family is. Family is not a contract among individuals, but the context within which persons have their identity constituted. The family precedes the individual. It is the first and vital cell of society. Society, in turn, is family blown large.

The mission of the family, according to John Paul, is to serve life and love. The family creates life, nourishes it across its cycles, and passes life on for future generations. The primary and irreplaceable expression of family is the procreation and education of children, set in a context of responsible fertility. But the role of the family does not stop there. The family also forms community and spins the web of community ever wider up to the human family. Families are to be communions of life and love, beginning in intimacy yet reaching out to society. The family needs, either singly or in associations, to devote itself to society, and especially to the poor. A first step in this work is to make sure that social policy grounds itself on the principle of family. In particular, proclaiming a declaration of the rights of family, and especially of its priority to the state, would be helpful. Because the social question today is global, the social mission of families itself takes on a global character.

Special attention is given in *Familiaris Consortio* to the role of men as well as women as spouses and parents (although the section on women is nearly three times the length of the section on men). Husbands and fathers are called to respect the equal dignity of their wives, to love their wives and children, to resist cultural tendencies that encourage the man to be less concerned with family, and, above all, to reject any oppressive role of *machismo* or a wrong superiority of male prerogatives. In contrast to *Laborem Exercens*, the man is not called the head of the family and is said to have responsibility for the children.

Women's equal dignity and responsibility for public life are noted, and society's failure to honor this equal dignity and responsibility is criticized. But the work of women outside the home is said to require clear recognition of the value of their maternal and family roles, by comparison with other public roles and professions. Society should be structured in such a way that wives and mothers need not work outside the home.

Married men and women are, therefore, proposed to have distinct vocations: women predominantly to the home, although not isolated from public life, and men predominantly to the world of work outside the home, but with a responsible presence in the home. There are also short sections on children and the elderly, but surprisingly no mention of grandparents, aunts, uncles, cousins, and ancestors. Finally, there is a reference to a fundamental bond between work and family, but it is not explained.

III. TOWARD DIALOGUE

I have, thus far, set an analytical context for and then outlined, by means of his teaching on the role of the laity in society, Pope John Paul II's conservative exploration of a postmodern vision. Having done that, I want now to suggest some areas where a dialogue between John Paul and the liberal American exploration of the postmodern vision might be fruitful.

John Paul's Offerings

In my opinion, John Paul is fundamentally correct in his analysis of the destructive course of modern culture, including modern American culture; in his prediction of the potential birth of a postmodern culture; in his criticism of modernity's tendency to repress the female symbol and to approach everything in terms of the masculine symbol; and in his interpretation of the outcome of this reductionism, namely the loss of spiritual energy, the erosion of family and community, the degradation of work, and the fundamental threat to the biosphere.

John Paul therefore brings many themes for dialogue to liberal American postmodernists. These include defense of family as more fundamental than contractual individualism, labor as the source of work's creativity, a global perspective, the public role of cultural and spiritual symbols, defense of the feminine symbol as life-bearing, and the danger of privatized consumerist ideology.

American Offerings

American culture, especially its liberal postmodern wing, also brings themes for dialogue to John Paul. The most obvious one is the interpretation of the sexual symbols and their spiritual, ecological, and social implications. There are major differences between John Paul's proposal for a postmodern vision and the postmodern vision arising within the liberal wing of American culture.

The liberal American stream of the postmodern vision does not see the solution to these spiritual, ecological, and social problems in a restoration of the classical European hierarchical/dualistic interpretation of the sexual symbols. For the classical view, as already developed, the male and female symbols are understood in the framework of a hierarchical dualism, with the male representing the Divine and the female representing human receptivity to Divine transcendence, with the transcendent/receptive (male/female) pattern repeated in the history/nature relationship, and with work linked to history and family to nature. By contrast, the liberal American postmodern stream proposes a legal equality of the sexes, and tends to place the feminine symbols in a central role for the signification of Divinity, humanity, and nature.

This liberal American postmodern stream is grounded scientifically and spiritually in a fresh, postmodern, developmental/holistic cosmology quite different from the chain-of-being image of classical European cosmology and its classical understanding of biological reproduction. Again, the classical chain of being functioned only according to a top-down framework of transcendence, and saw the feminine sexual partner only as a receptive nest for the male to generate life. It began with a vision of God as symbolically masculine, transcending humanity from above, then proceeded to humanity as dominating transcendentally over nature from above, and only finally arrived at nature as the totally transcended. By contrast, the liberal American postmodern perspective proceeds only from the bottom up in a framework of immanence, adds the dimension of God as symbolically feminine giving life from below, proceeds to the unfolding creativity of the universe's ecological dynamism, and finally comes to humanity as an emerging consciousness within nature, all perceived in a framework of ecological, human, Divine communion.

The American perspective also suggests that not only are there problematic areas in the modern Western scientific tradition, but that these problematic areas are rooted in the classical European spiritual tradition's imbalanced preoccupation with the male symbol of transcendence as exclusively imaging the Divine, in turn failing to honor sufficiently the female symbol of immanence as an equally important and complementary revelation of the Divine.

A Third Position?

Might it be that the contrast of these liberal and conservative visions of postmodern culture, embodied in the above contrasts, still carry the symbolic sibling rivalry of modern culture? And yet, there appears to be a paradoxical reversal of positions. In modern culture, prior to its crisis, the religious side stressed the feminine principle, while the scientific side stressed the masculine principle. But now the conservative religious stream is stressing the masculine symbol, while the liberal secular stream is stressing the feminine symbol.

Might there yet be a third position in which the male and female symbols are viewed as complementary partners, both revealing dimensions of the Divine and its revelation in the unfolding universe and its human species?

Might this be what Genesis 1:27 means when it links the image of God with the creation of male and female? Are not both the male and female symbols needed fully to image the Divine? Do not the masculine and feminine symbols express together the ecological creativity of the universe? Are they perhaps now coming to a new depth and risk with the unfolding of human consciousness?

From this third perspective, the male and female symbols would not be separated in a predominantly male world of work (outside the home) and a predominantly female world of family (with its own work). The social experience would not be defined exclusively in the feminine cyclical and nurturing mode, or in the masculine innovative and achieving mode. A new complementarity of female and male technologies and of the female and male symbols would instead emerge (even though individuals from both sexes span a spectrum of skills and tendencies). There would then emerge a fresh female and male partnership of equal, complementary, and creative communion within work and family, as well as in the reconnecting of the two. History and nature would no longer be distinct or antagonistic.

From the perspective of this third position, the social task would not be simply the conservative prescription to use the classical European spiritual tradition of masculine transcendence to correct the modern scientific project. Nor would it be simply the liberal prescription to reject outright our classical heritage and to forget any unique and indispensable function for the masculine symbol. Neither strategy alone would seem to bring radical healing. The broader strategy would be to bring both to create, together, an authentically postmodern, holistic healing of the complementary immanent/transcendent mutuality of the sexual symbols across the ecological, human, and Divine communion of cocreativity.

For this view, such healing would mean asserting neither the primacy of transcendence over immanence, nor the primacy of immanence over transcendence, but rather an embrace of the two. This embrace would free the male symbol and masculine technologies from their flight from woman, sexuality and nature (expressed as the desire to dominate, control, and ultimately to repress the feminine disclosure of the Divine). It would also free the female symbol to come forth into the center of the social world, bringing its healing and life-giving power by discovering the humanness of the male symbol, thereby overcoming any intimidation by it, and bringing the gift of feminine unifying and cyclical technologies into the heart of the social project.

CONCLUSION

Pope John Paul II, as a leading conservative thinker grounded in the masculine principle of transcendence, has begun a creative retrieval of the classical European heritage and placed it at the service of a still unknown postmodern global culture. This effort needs to be distinguished from the late modern neoconservative attempt to use the classical masculine heritage to reinforce the legitimacy of threatened modern ideologies, in our case the capitalist ideology.

Similarly, many liberal American thinkers, grounded in the feminine principle of immanence, have begun a creative retrieval of our primal roots as a step toward creation of a postmodern culture. This effort needs to be distinguished from the late modern attempt to employ feminine energies in the service of modern ideologies, again in our case the capitalist ideology.

A next step for both these efforts is to see if they have something to give each other. Leaving behind all residues of modern culture's sibling rivalry, the result could be the fertile embrace of a postmodern creative communion capable of healing the deep ecological, social, and spiritual crisis of modern culture. The rivals would become lovers, and from the union of the two would come a child—the regeneration of life beyond the deadly threat of the modern crisis.

NOTES

1. I use the term *liberal* broadly to refer to all modern ideologies that give primacy to the themes of freedom and progress, that is, to the progressive emancipation of the self from the tradition and authority of received community, in contrast to premodern conservative ideologies, which give priority to the themes of authority and tradition and so contain the self within their boundaries.

2. Charles Jencks, the main definer of postmodern architecture and an analyst of the postmodern movement in the visual arts and literature, describes the movement as embracing a synthesis of past and present traditions. He distinguishes what he sees as authentically postmodern from other tendencies that are labelled *postmodern* but are in his view only late modern, such as minimalism in art, high tech in architecture, and deconstruction in philosophy. See Charles Jencks, *What Is Post-Modernism?* (New York: St. Martin's Press, 1987).

3. Simone Weil, *The Need for Roots,* trans. Arthur Wills (Boston: Beacon Press, 1952). A Jew by birth, Weil was drawn toward Catholicism.

4. See, for example, the multiple references in John Paul II's September 14, 1981 encyclical, *Laborem Exercens.* The official English translation can be found in *Origins: NC Documentary Service* 11/15 (September 24, 1981), 225-44.

5. "As Pope Confronts Dissenters, Whose Catholicism Will Prevail?" *New York Times,* December 23, 1986, A1, A8.

6. Richard John Neuhaus, *The Catholic Moment: The Paradox of the Church in the Postmodern World* (San Francisco: Harper & Row, 1987).

7. For the full text, see John Paul II, *Sollicitudo Rei Socialis,* which is found in *Origins: NC Documentation Service* 17/38 (March 3, 1988), 641-60. For confirmation of the Pope's anticapitalist stance, and his willingness to draw on important

insights from liberation theology (which Neuhaus firmly opposes), see the analysis by Roberto Suro, Rome correspondent for the *New York Times,* of the drafting of the encyclical, "The Writing of *Sollicitudo Rei Socialis*: A Behind-the-Scenes Account," in *Crisis* 6/5 (May 1988), 13–18.

8. This entire section, with minor modifications, is excerpted from my essay, "The Conservative/Liberal Exploration of the Postmodern Stage of Human Culture," *Occasional Papers* (South Orange, N. J.: PILLAR, 1988).

9. See Thomas Berry, "The Ecological Age," *Riverdale Papers* Vol. VI, 1–9 (these photocopied essays are available from The Riverdale Center for Religious Research, 5801 Palisade Avenue, Riverdale, N. Y. 10471); Marshall McLuhan, *Understanding Media: The Extension of Man* (New York: McGraw Hill, 1964); Erich Neumann, *The Origins and History of Consciousness* (Princeton, N. J.: Princeton University Press, 1970); and Gibson Winter, *Liberating Creation: Foundations of Religious Social Ethics* (New York: Crossroad Publishing Co., 1981).

10. On the Catholic principle of analogy, see David Tracy, *The Analogical Imagination: Christian Theology and the Culture of Pluralism* (New York: Crossroad Publishing Co., 1981). The classical Catholic statement of this complementarity was "grace builds on nature." A Catholic spirituality would, therefore, build on a natural spirituality, even while healing its distortions.

11. I learned this from Charlene Spretnak. See her *The Spiritual Dimension of Green Politics* (Santa Fe, N. M.: Bear & Co., 1986), 33–34.

12. Monica Sjoo and Barbara Mor, *The Great Cosmic Mother: Rediscovering the Religion of the Earth* (San Francisco: Harper & Row, 1987).

13. *Ibid.,* 7.

14. Stanley Jaki has argued that a sense of religious transcendence over the webs and cycles of nature, particularly during the Middle Ages, was a precondition for scientific development. See *The Origin of Science and the Science of its Origin* (South Bend, Ind.: Regnery/Gateway, 1978).

15. Umberto Eco, *The Name of the Rose*, trans. William Weaver (San Diego, Calif.: Harcourt Brace Jovanovich, 1983).

16. See Carolyn Merchant, *The Death of Nature: Women, Ecology, and the Scientific Revolution* (San Francisco: Harper & Row, 1980).

17. *Teilhard Studies*, No. 1 (New York: The American Teilhard Association for the Future of Man [867 Madison Avenue], n.d.).

18. For example, a recent study by Notre Dame University of English-speaking, white, Catholic parishes in the United States showed that, in terms of participation (rather than authority), parish life is mainly the domain of women, while civic life is mainly the domain of men. See David C. Leege, "Catholics in the Civic Order: Parish Participation, Politics, and Civic Participation," Report No. 11 of The Notre Dame Study of Catholic Parish Life (October 1987), 6.

19. C. P. Snow, *The Two Cultures and the Scientific Revolution* (New York: Cambridge University Press, 1961).

20. Robert Bellah, Richard Madsen, William M. Sullivan, Ann Swidler, and Steven M. Tipton, *Habits of the Heart: Individualism and Commitment in American Life* (New York: Harper & Row, 1985).

21. For interesting reflections (including video materials) on this process, see the work of William and Sylvia Everett in their *"Oikos* Project," from the Candler School of Theology, Emory University, Atlanta, Ga.

22. See John Bossey, "The Counter Reformation and the People of Catholic Europe," *Past and Present* 47 (1970), 51–70.

23. For reflection on the new scientific paradigm and the "Green" movement growing out of it, see Fritjof Capra, *The Turning Point: Science, Society, and the Rising Culture* (New York: Simon & Schuster, 1982); Brian Swimme, *The Universe Is a Green Dragon: A Cosmic Creation Story* (Santa Fe, N. M.: Bear & Co., 1985); and Fritjof Capra and Charlene Spretnak, *Green Politics: The Global Promise* (New York: E. P. Dutton, 1984).

24. A number of explorations of liberal postmodernism by thinkers with Catholic roots exist. Matthew Fox in *Original Blessing: A Primer in Creation Spirituality* (Santa Fe, N. M.: Bear & Co., 1983) appeals to hidden or recessive primal sources in the Christian mystical tradition, to Judaism, and to Native American spirituality. Charlene Spretnak in *The Spiritual Dimension of Green Politics* draws on her studies of European pre-Christian goddess mythology, Buddhism, the wisdom tradition of Christian mystics, Native American spirituality, and the contemporary "Green" movement. In a later essay, "The Regenerationist Perspective" (in Joe Holland and Anne Barsanti, eds., *American and Catholic: The New Debate* [South Orange, N. J.: PILLAR Books, 1988]), she suggests linkage between "Green" ecological principles and the Catholic social thought of Pope Pius XI's 1931 encyclical letter on the social question, *Quadragesimo Anno.* See also the work of Thomas Berry as addressed in Anne Lonergan & Caroline Richards, eds., *Thomas Berry and the New Cosmology* (Mystic, Conn.: Twenty Third, 1987). For an important religious exploration by an Episcopal theologian, see Gibson Winter, *Liberating Creation: Foundations of Religious Social Ethics.*

25. Joe Holland, "John Paul II on the Laity in Society: The Spiritual Transformation of Modern Culture," *Social Thought* 13/2–3 (Spring/Summer 1987), 87–103.

26. "Science and the Church in the Nuclear Age" (address to the European Center for Nuclear Research), *Origins: NC Documentation Service* 12:126–28.

27. In documenting the thought of John Paul II, I for the most part limit myself to readily available texts. Of special help in this regard is Leonard Doohan, ed., *John Paul II and the Catholic Laity* (LeJacq, 1984), which brings together excerpts from 273 sources of John Paul's writing or speaking. In addition, I do not try to document every statement offered here, which would require perhaps a thousand notes. Rather, I give each time a reference for broad areas of the text, and hope that the reader can, without much difficulty, find in the reference the appropriate location for precise statements.

28. Mary Craig, *Man from a Far Country: A Portrait of Pope John Paul II* (London: Hodder and Stoughton, 1979).

29. E. J. Dionne, "As Pope Confronts Dissenters, Whose Catholicism Will Prevail?" *New York Times*, December 23, 1986, A8.

30. John Paul II, "Science and the Church in the Nuclear Age."

31. John Paul II, *Sign of Contradiction* (London: Hodder and Stoughton, 1979), 156.

32. *Ibid.*, 51.

33. *Idem.*

34. *Ibid.*, 55-56, 124.

35. John Paul II, *Laborem Exercens*, 238-39.

36. John Paul II, *Sign of Contradiction*, 204-07.

37. John Paul II, "Science and the Church in the Nuclear Age" and "The Holy Spirit in the Church and in the World" (Encyclical Letter), *Origins: NC Documentation Service* 12:126-28 and 15:79-102.

38. John Paul II, *Sign of Contradiction*, 204-05.

39. John Paul II, "The Holy Spirit in the Church and in the World."

40. Doohan, ed., *John Paul II and the Catholic Laity*, 73.

41. *Ibid.*, 32; John Paul II, "Science and the Church in the Nuclear Age."

42. John Paul II, *Sign of Contradiction*, 19-26.

43. Doohan, ed., *John Paul II and the Catholic Laity*; John Paul II, *Laborem Exercens*.

44. Arthur O. Lovejoy, *The Great Chain of Being* (Cambridge, Mass.: Harvard University Press, 1964).

7

LIBERATION THEOLOGY AND POSTMODERN PHILOSOPHY: A RESPONSE TO CORNEL WEST

David Ray Griffin

I find Cornel West's developing theology[1] one of the most exciting and important ventures on the scene today. I share his conviction that modernity is dying, that this is good, and that we need a postmodern theology. I find, however, his own religious and philosophical vision in considerable tension with the philosophical tradition of postanalytic neopragmatism to which he nominally professes primary, if ambivalent, allegiance. I suggest that Whitehead's philosophy provides the basis for the kind of postmodern theology that is needed.

I. NIHILISTIC POSTMODERNISM AND MORAL NORMS

Although he is not uncritical of it, West identifies primarily with the neo-pragmatism of his teacher, Richard Rorty, and the "patriarchal trio of postmodern philosophers," Willard Quine, Nelson Goodman, and Wilfred Sellars, on which Rorty's program is primarily built (in spite of Rorty's crediting of Wittgenstein, Heidegger, and Dewey).[2] West says that it is a "tragedy" that most theologians do not know the Quine-Goodman-Sellars approach, and that it, in conjunction with Third World liberation theology, provides the best basis for a contemporary American theology.[3]

On the basis of this trio, West points out, Rorty has drawn three major consequences: a rejection of realistic ontology, with its correspondence theory of truth; a rejection of foundationalism, with its givenness and pre-linguistic awareness; and epistemological behaviorism, which dismisses the mind as a sphere of inquiry.[4] The fact that West regards this neopragmatic philosophical approach as so potentially important for theology is doubly puzzling. First, its conclusions do not provide support for West's major concerns. Second, his own evaluation of the consequences and failures of neopragmatism is extremely negative.

West regards the ethical point of view as central for pragmatists, and is above all concerned not only to have moral norms, but norms that can be justified.[5] Analytic neopragmatism, however, like most modern philosophy, equates perception with *sense*-perception, which rules out the possibility that moral values or norms could be given to experience. This approach also denies that *anything* is given to experience.[6] It is not clear how West, insofar as he accepts these presuppositions, could justify the moral norms that he affirms. He speaks of "condemning all forms of philosophical activity that devalue . . . alternatives to prevailing practices" and that engage in the wholesale "trashing of standards."[7] But to condemn others for not having norms or standards is not to justify one's own.

West recognizes that moral visions and ethical norms flow from "synoptic world views," and that nihilistic relativism results from the lack of such worldviews.[8] He himself points out that the neopragmatists have failed to provide a new worldview,[9] and this failure is not merely fortuitous. This form of postmodern thought, with its antirealist and antifoundational positions, rules out *in principle* the development or endorsement of a synoptic worldview. This philosophical defect cannot be overcome by the proposed marriage with liberation theologies, at least on West's analysis of them, because they are regarded as "lacking in serious philosophical substance."[10] Thus, neither of the two marriage partners brings the needed dowry.

West wants a theology that supports liberation. Rorty and some of the other members of this tradition, however, affirm behaviorism and eliminative materialism,[11] both of which try to eliminate language about human experience. Eliminative materialism tries to avoid the problem of how to relate physicalistic language about neural events to mentalistic language about emotions, sensory data, and the like, by eliminating the latter, translating it into statements about neural events. This materialistic and behavioristic approach prevents any philosophical justification for concern about the quality of human experience. Not only its nihilistic implications, but West's own negative evaluation of this form of postmodern thought makes his formal allegiance to it strange. Its only accomplishment, in his view, was to correct some errors that had been imported into American philosophy from European logical positivism, errors that the earlier American pragmatic and process traditions, as he sees, had avoided all along. [12] Furthermore, although West tries valiantly to portray Rorty and the Quine-Goodman-Sellars trinity as a significant recovery of American pragmatism, [13] he also portrays them as devoid of virtually everything that he values in pragmatism. While he believes that "American philosophy at its best has taken the form of philosophy of religion," he points out that neopragmatism has little interest in religious reflection, being preoccupied instead with what he calls the secular priesthood of modern culture, the scientific community. [14] Because these philosophers have not taken religion seriously, he says, they have not taken culture and society seriously, providing no sustained social and cultural criticism. [15] This form of philosophy has no ethical consequences for society, West believes, and is of no interest beyond philosophy departments. [16] How then can this tradition be called *neopragmatism*, as if it were a significant recovery of the spirit of American pragmatism? West's evaluation becomes even more negative; he says that this "post-modern American philosophy—similar to much of post-modern thought in the West—constitutes a dead, impotent rhetoric of a declining and decaying civilization." [17] The viewpoints of Quine, Goodman, Sellars, and Rorty "leave post-modern American philosophy hanging in limbo, as a philosophically critical yet culturally lifeless rhetoric mirroring a culture (or civilization) permeated by the scientific ethos, regulated by racist, patriarchal, capitalist norms, and pervaded by debris of decay." [18]

One might suspect that West's ability to praise this philosophy's potential so highly while viewing its results so negatively is due to a failure to see that its results flow from its basic principles. But this is not so. West realizes clearly that its nihilism follows from its "anti-realism, conventionalism, relativism, and anti-foundationalism." [19] This evaluation leaves me puzzled how West's positive and negative evaluations of this form of postmodernism can be combined.

He evidently thinks that the norms and the concomitant synoptic worldview for which he sees a need can be had without metaphysical support, at least if metaphysics is understood to involve ahistorical, transcendental criteria, which he rejects. [20] These criteria, I take it, include coherence and adequacy to the facts of experience. The latter criterion would be eliminated, of course, by the antifoundationalist denial that a distinction can be made between the given (or factual) and interpretive elements of experience.

How would West, without a metaphysically supported vision, escape relativism so as to affirm and justify a moral vision with its norms? He speaks of reaffirming the moral visions and ethical norms of "the best of available religious and secular traditions bequeathed to us from the past."[21] How can there be a noncircular determination of which of those traditions is "the best"? For West, the best is the prophetic Christian tradition.[22] His acceptance of this tradition, he says, "is rational in that it rests upon good reasons."[23] How can particular reasons be called "good," however, if the traditional metaphysical criteria for judging a position true cannot be applied? West expresses confidence in "sound human judgment relative to the most rationally acceptable theories and descriptions of the day."[24] But does not this statement presuppose some criterion for judging which theories are "the most rationally acceptable"? West says that we should scrutinize synoptic worldviews in terms of two criteria. The first criterion for worldviews is "their comprehensive grasp of the complexity, multiplicity, and specificity of human experiences." This criterion seems to include the criterion of adequacy to the facts of experience. The second criterion is "their enabling power to motivate human action for the negation and transformation of structures of oppression."[25] This criterion presupposes that we have some norms by which we can judge certain structures as "oppressive." West himself says that a philosophy fails if it cannot justify moral norms. But how can he hope to provide justification for norms within the framework of a philosophy that disallows any nonsensory intuition of norms or values, and explicitly rejects any nonculturally-conditioned *given* element in experience by which the currently dominant norms can be challenged as inadequate?

At the center of West's concern for "negation and transformation" is the notion of "new possibilities, potentialities, and alternatives to present practices."[26] The kind of philosophy with which he has verbally aligned himself is, however, devoid of such a notion. Sensationist empiricisms characteristically reject the notion of alternative possibilities, or "counterfactuals," because these alleged entities cannot be perceived by the senses. Materialistic ontologies likewise reject the existence of "possibilities," because such entities would be nonmaterial, and because materialism usually implies determinism.

My point is that West cannot rest content with purely pragmatic criteria for judging a worldview. These criteria can themselves only be justified by appeal to metaphysical ideas. In West's theology thus far, this appeal has remained implicit. The radical contradiction between this appeal and the so-called neopragmatic philosophy of Rorty has thereby been obscured.

II. TRUTH, CORRESPONDENCE, AND GIVENNESS

West's difficulty, as I have analyzed it, is that he gives formal allegiance to a philosophical tradition that is deeply alien, not only in its development thus far but in its basic principles, to his own substantive vision. In this section, I examine those basic principles to see if any good reason exists for West to consider them to be established beyond revision or even to be appropriate in our present historical situation.

At the heart of the conventionalism and relativism of this nihilistic postmodern philosophy is a rejection of the correspondence theory of truth, which is supported by a rejection of any preinterpretive "given" element in experience. West seems to accept this twofold rejection.[27]

As a pragmatist, however, West presumably accepts William James' dictum that it makes no sense to reject an idea if one cannot actually live in terms of that rejection. This dictum is the pragmatic rephrasing of the principle of commonsense philosophers, that the ultimate criteria for philosophy are those ideas that are so fundamental that their truth must be implicitly affirmed in the very attempt to deny them. Whitehead formulates this criterion as "the metaphysical rule of evidence: that we must bow to those presumptions, which, in despite of criticism, we still employ for the regulation of our lives."[28] We should never, he says, accept the adequacy of "negations of what in practice is presupposed."[29]

The idea that the very meaning of *truth* is the correspondence between a proposition and the thing(s) to which it refers appears to be an ultimate presumption which is implicitly affirmed in every attempt to deny it. For example, West quotes the following passage by Thomas Kuhn (called, along with Rorty, a "renegade stepchild" of Goodman and Quine):

A scientific theory is usually felt to be better than its predecessors . . . because it is somehow a better representation of what nature is really like. One often hears that successive theories grow ever closer to, or approximate more and more closely to, the truth. Apparently generalizations like that refer . . . to [the theory's] ontology, to the match, that is, between the entities with which the theory populates nature and what is 'really there'. . . . There is, I think, no theory-independent way to reconstruct phrases like 'really there'; the notion of a match between the ontology of a theory and its 'real' counterpart in nature now seems to me illusive in principle.[30]

Kuhn appears to reject the notion of truth as correspondence between theory and reality. Yet he presupposes it in every sentence. In the first, he tells us what is "usually felt" about scientific theories. His statement is true if and only if it corresponds to the feelings of most people who think about these matters. Or take the last sentence: it is true if and only if his theory about what is not possible in principle corresponds to the real situation. (Of course, it *cannot* so correspond, or the theory would be both true and false.) The point can be illustrated by one of West's own passages.

> [C]rucial philosophical debates are less about the way the world is . . . and more about how self-critical interlocutors . . . project and preserve regulative self-images and guiding vocabularies that promote various aims and purposes. For example, the basic aim of philosophical realists in our time is to defend what some authoritative institutional practices, e.g., those of the scientific community or of some religious community, say that the world really is. . . . For both types of realists (secular or religious), it is Reality which ultimately serves as the arbiter of which theories or interpretations are accepted and warranted.
>
> For historicists, secular realism is an intellectual strategy adopted by those who promote the authority of the secular priesthood. . . .[31]

West is denying the realist's claim that debates are about the way the world is. West tells us, however, the way the (human) world really is. His statement is true if and only if his theory about the aim of realists corresponds to the basic aim (conscious or unconscious) that actually motivates their philosophical writings. That West's theory is about human aims rather than natural processes makes it no less realistic in intention. And if his realist theory about realists is true, then his own aim as a realist is to defend some authoritative institutional practice. If his basic aim is to do that, however, instead of describing what realists are really like, why should we pay attention to him? Et cetera, et cetera.

Something is clearly amiss. West denies that he accepts the correspondence theory of truth, yet he obviously presupposes what I mean by that theory. The problem is that *he includes as an essential component of the theory an element that I do not include*, the idea that there can be theory-independent observation-statements. To make this idea an essential element of the correspondence theory of the *meaning* truth is to equate the meaning of an idea with its mode of verification—which is to hold onto one of the pillars of the logical positivism which West means to reject. This equation of meaning and verification seems to be expressed in the following passage, in which West exegetes Rorty:

> To put it crudely, ideas, words, and language are not mirrors which copy the 'real' or 'objective' world but rather tools with which we cope with 'our' world.
>
> In a more philosophical vein . . . the theory-laden character of observations relativizes talk about the world such that realist appeals to 'the world' as a final court of appeal to determine what is true can only be viciously circular. We cannot isolate 'the world' from theories of the world, then compare these theories of the world with a theory-free world.[32]

To hold to the correspondence *meaning* of truth, however, does not require one to hold this naive idea of how to *test* a proposition. The two ideas certainly are not connected in Whitehead's thought.

For Whitehead, the *correspondence theory* of truth applies only to the *meaning* of the truth and falsehood of propositions, not to the *testing* of a judgment about a proposition. A proposition is a theory about particular actualities. It is either true or false all by itself, independently of whether it is thought to be true by anyone, that is, independently of how it is entertained in a propositional feeling by anyone.[33] A proposition is a unique kind of entity, distinct from actualities and pure possibilities (eternal objects). It is in fact "a hybrid between pure potentialities and actualities."[34] The actualities constitute the logical subjects of the proposition, the pure potentialities (eternal objects) constitute the predicate. "The proposition is the possibility of *that* predicate applying in that assigned way to *those* logical subjects."[35] The proposition is true if the nexus of actualities constituting the logical subjects "does in reality exemplify the pattern which is the predicate of the proposition."[36] The proposition is true, in other words, if it corresponds to reality.

In what sense can a proposition, which is a possibility, "correspond" to a nexus of actualities? Bishop Berkeley said that an idea can only correspond to another idea. Obviously, a theory and the fact to which it refers cannot be identical. The two *are* identical, insofar as the theory is true, in one respect; they both involve the same eternal objects, or pure potentialities. But they differ in the *mode of togetherness* of these eternal objects:

> The nexus includes the eternal object in the mode of realization. Whereas in the true proposition the togetherness of the nexus and the eternal object belongs to the mode of abstract possibility. . . . Thus a nexus and a proposition belong to different categories of being. Their identification is mere nonsense.

This doctrine, by pointing out that correspondence does not mean identity, provides a partial answer to Berkeley. But the reference to Berkeley raises a deeper question. He used the principle that an idea can refer only to another idea to reject the materialistic view of nature and to support his own idealistic view that nature consists merely of ideas impressed upon our minds by the divine mind. Being a personal rather than an absolute idealist, however, Berkeley believed in finite minds or spirits, which are fully actual, and that we can make true statements about them. Having stipulated that an idea can refer only to another idea, he said that we could have true "notions" about other minds. Here he granted that a theory could correspond with an actuality. As we have seen, West and those to whom he refers assume that they can make statements about other human subjects that can in principle be true, such as statements about their aims. They therefore agree with Berkeley that we can entertain true "notions." They have trouble with the idea of correspondence primarily with regard to statements about (nonhuman) nature. Not agreeing with Berkeley's view of nature as comprised only of ideas, believing instead (rightly) that the natural world is actual, they cannot see how ideas can correspond to it.

What is the relevant difference? My ideas (ignoring from now on Berkeley's distinction between notions and ideas) about other minds can be thought capable of corresponding to reality, because the reality in question is, like myself, an experiencing subject which can entertain ideas. I can assume that my theory about another person's aims or sense-data might correspond to that person's reality, because that person is thought to be the kind of entity that can have aims and see colors. But how could a theory about nature understood as comprised of (insentient) bits of matter be thought to correspond to it? It cannot. A bit of matter, by definition, is incapable of incorporating ideas.

It is this materialistic view of nature, and therefore the dualistic view of the relation between experience and nature (still presupposed by those who verbally espouse materialism), that seems to be the main reason in modern philosophy for the rejection of the correspondence theory of truth. As Whitehead says:

> All metaphysical theories which admit a disjunction between the component elements of individual experience on the one hand, and on the other hand the component elements of the external world, must inevitably run into difficulties over the truth and falsehood of propositions. . . .[38]

Because Whitehead rejects this disjunction, holding instead that there is no meaning to "togetherness" other than "experiential togetherness,"[39] he can define correspondence as he does. Rejecting dualism in favor of panexperientialism, he says that the entities constituting nature *can* embody some of the same ideas or eternal objects that enter into our own experience and that constitute the predicates of our theories about natural things.

It might be thought unfortunate that the correspondence theory of truth can be defended only by appeal to a particular ontology and a highly controversial one at that. The correspondence theory of truth, however, has been thrown into question by appeal to a particular ontology. And this dualistic (at least crypto-dualistic) ontology is discredited by (among other things) the fact that it cannot make intelligible the correspondence theory of truth, which the advocates of this ontology cannot help presupposing. (Incidentally, neither the correspondence theory of truth nor the ontology of panexperientialism should seem alien to those standing in the pragmatic tradition, because William James affirmed them both.)[40]

The Whiteheadian account of the meaning of truth as correspondence applies to propositions, it should be stressed, not to judgments. It involves only the question of what it *means* to say that a proposition is true or false, not also the epistemological question of how to test whether a particular proposition is true. The latter question presupposes the former, but is not presupposed by it. When Whitehead turns to this epistemological question, he does not speak naively about comparing theories with the world as it is in itself, apart from our interpretive experience of it. Has indeed any serious philosopher spoken in this naive way, or is this a straw-position created by those who reject correspondence? In any case, when Whitehead speaks of testing, he speaks of "pragmatic" tests and of "coherence."[41]

Thus far, I have argued the defensibility of one account of the correspondence theory of truth by (1) pointing out that it refers only to meaning, not also to testing, (2) showing that the correspondence theory in this sense is presupposed even by those who verbally reject it, (3) distinguishing correspondence from identity, and (4) showing how Whitehead's ontology makes the idea of correspondence intelligible with regard to propositions about things besides other human minds. The correspondence account presupposes a fifth idea, the idea of *givenness*, which is rejected by most of the postmodern philosophers to which West refers. Unless our experience is thought to refer beyond itself to something that is not its own creation, the idea that our theories correspond to a reality beyond themselves would be meaningless. In Whitehead's words: "The logical subjects of a proposition supply the element of givenness requisite for truth and falsehood."[42]

I said earlier that Whitehead rejects, with West and company, theory-free observation-statements. I say now, however, that Whitehead affirms a preinterpretive element of givenness in experience. To see how Whitehead's two beliefs are consistent, we need to distinguish three questions. First, can theory-neutral observation-statements be made? Second, does preinterpretive conscious perception occur? Third, is any element in experience given to it, prior to its interpretive response?

West and his philosophers do not clearly distinguish these three questions. They accordingly use negative answers to the first two questions, which are justified, as sufficient reason to reject givenness in the third and therefore *any* sense as a "myth."[43] West, for example, says that he "rejects Reality as the ultimate standard since reality-claims are theory-laden, i.e., our truth-claims are mediated by our theories."[44] This statement reflects a negative answer to the first question, about theory-neutral observation-statements. Sometimes West refers simply to "the theory-laden character of observations."[45] Because he and his philosophers are referring to conscious sense-perception, he is thereby giving a negative answer to the second question, whether we can have theory-neutral conscious perceptions. He goes on, however, to endorse the denial that "there is a given element—a . . . theory-neutral, noninferential element—in experience which . . . serves as the final terminating point for chains of epistemic justification."[46]

This conclusion follows from negative answers to the first two questions only if the third question cannot be intelligibly distinguished from them. That would be the case if there were no prelinguistic experience and no preconscious, presensory experience. Wilfred Sellars indeed builds his case against "the myth of the given" on the denial of prelinguistic experience.[47] But West, agreeing (in conversation) that dogs and babies have experience, accepts prelinguistic experience. West's philosophers, like virtually all modern philosophers, also equate perception with *sense*-perception. Even aside from the evidence for what is normally called extrasensory perception, however, good reasons exist to reject this equation, as Whitehead shows. Because he rejects the modern denial of nonsensory and nonlinguistic experience, Whitehead can agree with the antifoundationalists on the first two questions while giving a positive answer to the third, regarding a preinterpretive, given element in experience. More space in his writings is, in fact, devoted to the clarification and justification of this point than to any other issue. I will summarize his position, which is difficult but crucial.

Whitehead distinguishes between three modes of perception. The most obvious form is called *perception in the mode of presentational immediacy* because some data, usually sense-data, are immediately present to one's consciousness. Hume and most other modern philosophers have considered this the sole form of perception. But, for Whitehead, it is always an abstraction from complete human perception, which is *perception in the mixed mode of symbolic reference.*[48] In this mixed mode, the pure mode of presentational immediacy is combined with the other pure mode, *perception in the mode of causal efficacy.* Causal efficacy is the most primordial mode of perception, the mode we share with all other actual things. It is in this mode that the past world of actual things is *given* to us. It is called *causal efficacy* because the other things are perceived as actual and as thereby exerting causal efficacy upon the perceiver. Through this perception of givenness we know about William James' "stubborn fact" which cannot be avoided.[49] Even the most extreme solipsist gets out of the way when he sees an automobile bearing down upon him.

Although we all behave in practice in accord with the knowledge that our experience contains given elements which we did not create, it is, Whitehead comments, "in respect to this 'stubborn fact' that the theories of modern philosophy are weakest."[50] The reason is that modern philosophers have focused almost exclusively on perception in the mode of presentational immediacy, in which no actuality with causal power is given. They have ignored perception in the mode of causal efficacy.[51] The reason for this malign neglect, according to Whitehead's account of perception, is that conscious experience, with which philosophy necessarily begins, usually illuminates presentational immediacy vividly but causal efficacy only dimly. It does this because perception in the mode of causal efficacy occurs at the outset of an occasion of experience, while consciousness occurs only at the end. It therefore sheds most of its light on presentational immediacy, which is also a latecomer.[52] This fact, combined with the assumption that the clearest elements in consciousness are the most fundamental (an assumption for which there is little excuse in a post-Freudian age), explains why philosophers have neglected perception in the mode of causal efficacy, with its element of givenness.[53]

Whitehead's positive answer to the question about an element of givenness in perception is combined with a negative answer to the other two questions. He distinguishes between a *proposition*, which is a meaning, and any *linguistic statement* that tries to express that proposition.[54] Any set of words used to express a proposition presupposes a whole system of language.[55] Any such system implies a worldview, which has been built on the basis of centuries of human interpretation. Theory-neutral observation-statements are therefore impossible. For example, in 1929, some four decades before the writings of Thomas Kuhn and Paul Feyerabend on this topic, Whitehead said:

> Our habitual experience is a complex of failure and success in the enterprise of interpretation. If we desire a record of uninterpreted experience, we must ask a stone to record its autobiography. Every scientific memoir in its record of the 'facts' is shot through and through with interpretation.[56]

This doctrine is now commonplace.

A second and less obvious point is that conscious perceptions already involve interpretations, or at least created elements. Insofar as consciousness presupposes perception in the mode of symbolic reference, it involves interpretation, because *symbolic reference* means that data from one mode of perception are used to interpret data from the other mode. For example, the colored shapes perceived in presentational immediacy are used to interpret the feeling of causal derivation from the eye, and also the dimmer feeling of derivation from the external world beyond the eye.

Even if one inhibits this natural interpretation, so that one focuses on the data of presentational immediacy themselves in abstraction from their role in symbolic reference, an element of creative origination is still involved. Not all philosophers have granted this. For example, West quotes H. H. Price's attempt to justify belief in givenness with reference to the perception of a tomato:

> One thing however I cannot doubt: that there exists a red patch of a round and somewhat bulky shape, standing out from a background of other colour patches, and having a certain visual depth, and that this whole field of colour is directly present to my consciousness. . . . This peculiar manner of being present to consciousness is called *being given* and that which is thus present is called a *datum*.[57]

Whitehead agrees that one cannot doubt that one sees what one sees, as long as one sticks solely to the phenomenal qualities of perception in the mode of presentational immediacy. He does not think, however, that these qualities, because indubitable, are thereby *given*, at least in the sense of givenness that is requisite for truth as correspondence. Rather, these phenomenal qualities are in part produced by the experiencing subject. The eternal object red, *as we see it* (that is, as a sense-datum qualifying a particular region of our visual field), does not arise in the receptive phase of an occasion of experience. It arises instead "from one of the originative phases of the percipient occasion."[58] It is, therefore, correct to call red *as we see it* a "secondary quality."[59]

Both parts of Whitehead's doctrine—that the sensory data that are prominent in consciousness are *created* by the experiencing subject, but that this creation is a transmutation of *given* elements—are summarized in the following passage:

> [T]he perceptive mode of presentational immediacy arises in the later, originative, integrative phases of the process of conscrescence. . . . [W]e must assign the mode of causal efficacy to the fundamental constitution of an occasion . . . ; while the mode of presentational immediacy requires the more sophistical activity of the later stages of process. . . . Presentational immediacy is an outgrowth from the complex datum implanted by causal efficacy.[60]

Whitehead, therefore, agrees with antifoundationalists that there are no theory-neutral observation-statements, that most conscious perception involves an interpretive judgment, and that all conscious perception involves elements that are not simply given. He maintains, nevertheless, that experience contains a given element. To a great extent, this givenness is perceived unconsciously. It is possible, however, to be consciously aware of this givenness. The conscious awareness of perception in the mode of causal efficacy, and therefore, of its given element, is usually vague and dim, but not always. Our memory, and our perception of the causal efficacy of our bodies for our conscious experience, provide the clearest examples. With regard to the latter, Whitehead points out repeatedly that Hume, in the very midst of denying that we have any direct conscious awareness of the existence of actualities beyond the ego and of their causal efficacy for the ego, mentions that we see *by means of the eye*.[61] With regard to memory: unless we groundlessly assume the existence of an enduring mind that remains numerically self-identical through time, memory is an example of the direct perception by our present moment of experience of something beyond itself—a previous moment of experience—and of its causal efficacy upon the present: "it remains remorselessly true, that we finish a sentence *because* we have begun it. We are governed by stubborn fact."[62]

The basic difference between Whitehead and the antifoundationalists is that the latter assume that perception is exhausted by sensory perception, while Whitehead recognizes a nonsensory type of perception. Memory and the direct perception of the causal efficacy of one's body are the two clearest examples of this nonsensory perception. When perception is restricted to sense-perception, denying an element of givenness is natural. Santayana, for example, refers to our belief in the existence of a real world as "animal faith," denying that the belief is based on the world's givenness. But this position means that the belief we all live by, that there is an actual world beyond ourselves which exerts causal power upon us, would have to be credited entirely, as Whitehead says, to "a primitive credulity."[63] West should prefer, I think, to rest his conviction in the existence of "sense-independent objects" on something else. The denial of the dogma of sensationism allows our belief in an objective world to be based upon a direct nonsensory perception of it.

This recognition of an element of givenness in experience allows us to justify an essential ingredient in the correspondence theory of truth. The recognition, discussed earlier, that this theory is simply a theory about meaning, not about verification, removes the other major objection that West's philosophers had raised about it. The adoption of panexperientialism—the only nondualistic view of the actual world that does not lead to behaviorism and eliminative materialism—removes the final ground in modern philosophy for opposing a correspondence theory of truth.

A direct connection exists between this set of issues and the issue that is at the heart of West's concern, the affirmation and justification of norms or values. The adoption of a nonsensationist epistemology allows us to affirm an element of givenness in our consciousness of moral and aesthetic norms. Recognition of an element of givenness with regard to ideals does not entail that they are *simply* received, of course, any more than recognizing a given element in our perception of actualities requires a naive realism. The assumption that our ideals of truth, beauty and goodness involve both given and constructed elements seems to fit the mix of universality and diversity that is revealed by a survey of human ideals.

The panexperientialist ontology, which allows us to make sense of the correspondence theory of truth, and the nonsensationist epistemology, which this ontology presupposes and implies, allow us to make sense of another belief that has been fundamental to biblically-based visions of reality. This is the twofold idea that God is directly experienced by human beings and that God is providentially active throughout the creation. The former belief is important for West's reaffirmation of the prophetic Christian tradition, the latter for his interest in enlarging this tradition to include a concern for ecological liberation.[64]

III. A DIFFERENT POSTMODERN CONTEXT

I have suggested that Whitehead's philosophy provides a much better basis for West's interests than does the postanalytic form of postmodernism to which he has given verbal if ambivalent allegiance. I now add the suggestion that Whitehead's philosophy can more meaningfully be called *postmodern*.

One anomaly in West's writing is that his use of *postmodern* is not commensurate with his characteristic use of *modern*. At one place, he defines modernity as a historical condition of abundant wealth resulting from the industrial-technological revolution, and of isolation, fragmentation, emptiness, sterility, and hypocrisy resulting from the disintegration of communities and religions.[65] Elsewhere he says that the modern world is based on science, subjectivist philosophy, classical aesthetic ideals, and the will to power, especially the will to cognition and control.[66] These descriptions portray modernity as a large-scale movement that arose in the seventeenth century. One would expect *postmodern philosophy* to refer to a form of philosophy that would challenge the basic presuppositions of this modern period. When West speaks of postmodern philosophy, however, the modernity that is in view seems to be much narrower. Modern philosophy seems to mean "modern analytic philosophy," especially logical positivism.[67] Given this meaning, a philosophy only has to overcome the problems peculiar to the logical positivism of the early part of the twentieth century to merit the term *postmodern*.[68]

A philosophy properly called postmodern (I claim) should address the problems of modern philosophy since the seventeenth century which have both reflected and contributed to the problems of modern culture. Two basic ingredients of modern philosophy are its sensationist epistemology and its materialistic, mechanistic view of nature. By the latter, I mean the view that the basic constituents of nature are devoid of any perception, or of any experience whatsoever, and devoid of any aim, any purposive or teleological element. The atoms, or elementary particles, are insentient, being only externally related to other atoms, and operate according to strictly mechanistic principles. In the first stage of modernity, this mechanistic account of nature was part of a dualistic account of the created world, in which these material particles were contrasted with the human soul, which had exactly the opposite attributes. In the second stage of modernity, dualism was verbally renounced in favor of full-fledged materialism, although this renunciation was never complete because no one could doubt that he or she had experiences. Even the eliminative materialists know what they are eliminating. Materialism is only dualism in disguise.

Insofar as the problems unique to the modern world are due to ideas, they are due mainly to these ideas and their implications. The atomistic ontology and the sensationist (solipsistic) epistemology led to perceived and actual isolation. Fragmentation was promoted both by the dualistic division of the world into bodies and minds, thereby its study into the sciences and the humanities, and by the sensationist epistemology, which removed values from the realm of cognition, thereby preventing synoptic worldviews in which science could be integrated with religion, aesthetics, and morality. Science alone was said to give real knowledge. This undermining of the cognitive basis for religious, ethical, and aesthetic ideas promoted the disintegration of religious traditions and in general contributed to the emptiness and sterility of modern life and left no normative checks on the will to power. The postanalytic thought that West calls *postmodern* does nothing to overcome the problems he has identified as distinctively modern. It in fact increases them, given its antifoundationalism, solipsism, and nihilism. Rather than challenging the basic tenets of modern philosophy, this postanalytic philosophy simply carries them to their logical conclusions, which were already seen by Hume and Nietzsche. It should be called *most*modern instead of postmodern. It is postmodern only in the sense of being the dead end of the modern trajectory. This is, in fact, West's own evaluation. He says that "postmodernism is an accentuation and acceleration of the major developments and processes of European modernism. It is a deepening of the decline of modernity with little sense of what is to follow, if anything at all."[69]

Whitehead's philosophy, by contrast, is postmodern in a more meaningful sense. With its panexperientialist ontology and nonsensationist epistemology, it challenges the basic tenets of the modern worldview. It thereby provides a basis for the correspondence theory of truth, for givenness, for a soul without dualism, and for the direct perception of God and of moral and aesthetic norms. This genuinely postmodern philosophy thus provides a basis for a theology that avoids nihilistic relativism without lapsing into a premodern form of metaphysics or revelationalism.

One final point. West stresses that an intellectual vision is utopian in the bad sense unless it "rests upon specifiable historical forces potentially capable of actualizing it."[70] In his own description of the postmodern world, he seems to accept Jean-François Lyotard's description of the postmodern condition as one in which "any sense of the whole has been lost."[71] This description no doubt describes a large segment of North American and European culture. This decadent form of postmodernism simply represents the final outworking in culture of the loss of wholeness that was implicit in the thought of the founders of the modern world, such as Descartes, Hobbes, Newton, and Hume.

In the midst of this decadence, however, one can discern the emergence of a fairly broad-based holistic movement that can be understood as a postmodern recovery of the premodern Renaissance holisms of the fifteenth, sixteenth, and seventeenth centuries, which were pushed underground as the modern worldview became dominant. This postmodernism looks less west (to Europe) than east (to Asia), back (to premodern thought), and down (to the depths of experience). It is also inspired by overlapping implications of the peace, ecology, and feminist movements and of recent developments in the sciences. The intellectual leadership of this postmodern movement includes physicists such as David Bohm, Brian Swimme, and Fritjof Capra; biologists such as Lewis Thomas, Rupert Sheldrake, and Charles Birch; psychologists such as James Hillman, Ken Wilber, and Rollo May; psychosomatic authors such as Kenneth Pelletier; parapsychologists such as Charles Tart, Stanley Krippner, and Kenneth Ring; social and cultural critics such as Robert Bellah and William Irwin Thompson; environmentalists such as Paul Ehrlich and Amory and Hunter Lovins; ecological feminists such as Charlene Spretnak, Carolyn Merchant, and Susan Griffin; spiritual writers such as Matthew Fox and Joanna Macy; agriculturalists such as Wendell Berry; political philosophers such as Richard Falk; poets such as Gary Snyder and Robert Bly; transdisciplinary thinkers such as Willis Harman, George Leonard, Norman Cousins, and Morris Berman;[72] as well as several philosophers and theologians. The broad base of the movement is shown by the popularity of these and similar authors and by the growth of various types of holistic publications. The general direction of this movement is in harmony with Whitehead's philosophy, as many of these leaders recognize.

Whether this movement provides the kind of social base that prevents holistic postmodern thought from being utopian in the bad sense depends upon one's assumption about how sociopolitical change occurs. Richard Falk says that what is utopian with regard to the nuclear crisis is to hope that "the current crop of the world rulers can be persuaded to subscribe to a plan for global disarmament." The reason is that the "modern world picture," which as applicable to politics was set out by Machiavelli, "dominates the thinking and behavior of virtually every political leader of the world." Falk concludes that a necessary condition for overcoming the "old order of separate, warring sovereignties" is the spread of the holistic world picture, which he sees emerging today—and he lives in Princeton, New Jersey, not California! The spread of this vision will allow for the emergence of a new type of leader while undermining the power grounding of the modern world picture.[73]

I suggest, accordingly, that our attempt to revitalize the best elements of the Christian tradition need not be carried out in terms of a postmodern context understood as unremittingly hostile to these elements, an attempt that leads to a purely pragmatic justification of moral norms which is ultimately circular. We can instead understand our task of bringing the best elements of our heritage to bear on our global problems in terms of an emerging postmodern context that is supportive of these elements. In this context, our best moral intuitions are supported by our best rational (ontological and epistemological) reflection. If our culture indeed continues to become postmodern in this sense, theologians will be confronted with a radically new situation. Unlike religious thinkers in the modern world, we will not need to spend the bulk of our energies on apologetics (which is what most modern theologians have done in some form even if they denied it). Rather, we will be able to turn our attention primarily to overcoming the demonic myths and structures that threaten our planet's total destruction.

NOTES

1. Although, according to my own usage, West is a theologian, he has used the term *philosophy of religion* to describe his own work. This is because, I learned in conversation, he has understood *theology* to involve the interpretation of texts accepted as authoritative. But it seems less inappropriate to refer to his thought as theology. On the one hand, it is clearly something quite different from that analytic enterprise, disconnected from actual social forces and normative concerns, with which philosophy of religion has become largely identified in recent decades. On the other hand, many forms of theology in recent centuries have not been oriented around the interpretation of authoritative texts.

2. Cornel West, "Afterword: The Politics of American Neo-Pragmatism," in John Rajchman and Cornel West, eds., *Post-Analytic Philosophy* (New York: Columbia University Press, 1985), 259–75, esp. 262.

3. Cornel West, "The Historicist Turn in Philosophy of Religion," in Leroy Rouner, ed., *Knowing Religiously* (Vol. 7 of "Boston University Studies in Philosophy and Religion") (Notre Dame, Ind.: University of Notre Dame Press, 1985), 36–51, esp. 41, 45, 46.

4. "Afterword," 263–65.

5. *Ibid.*, 267; "The Historicist Turn," 45, 47; "Philosophy and the Afro-American Experience," *The Philosophical Forum* LX (Winter 1977–78), 117–48, esp. 122.

6. "Nietzsche's Prefiguration of Post-Modern Literature," *Boundary 2: A Journal of Post-Modern Literature* 9 & 10 (Spring/Fall 1981), 241–70, esp. 252–60.

7. "The Historicist Turn," 47.

8. *Ibid.*, 48, 49.

9. "Nietzsche's Prefiguration," 242, 265.

10. "The Historicist Turn," 45.

11. "Afterword," 265; "Nietzsche's Prefiguration," 261.

12. "The Historicist Turn," 38–41.

13. *Ibid.*, 42; "Afterword," 261, 266.

14. "The Historicist Turn," 45, 42.

15. *Ibid.*, 43, 46.

16. *Ibid.*, 43; "Afterword," 267–68.

17. "Nietzsche's Prefiguration," 242.

18. *Ibid.*, 265.

19. *Ibid.*, 265.

20. "The Historicist Turn," 46, 49.

21. *Ibid.*, 46.

22. *Ibid.*, 49.

23. *Ibid.*, 49.

24. *Ibid.*, 47.

25. *Ibid.*, 46.

26. *Ibid.*, 47.

27. "Nietzsche's Prefiguration," 243-52; "Philosophy and the Afro-American Experience," 118, 144.

28. Alfred North Whitehead, *Process and Reality*, corrected edition, ed. David Ray Griffin and Donald W. Sherburne (1929; New York: Free Press, 1978), 151.

29. *Ibid.*, 13.

30. "Nietzsche's Prefiguration," 247-48.

31. "Dispensing with Metaphysics in Religious Thought," *Religion & Intellectual Life* 3/3 (Spring 1986), 53-56.

32. "Afterword," 263-64.

33. Whitehead, *Process and Reality*, 258.

34. *Ibid.*, 184-85.

35. *Ibid.*, 258.

36. Whitehead, *Adventures of Ideas* (1933; New York: Free Press, 1967), 244.

37. *Idem.*

38. *Process and Reality*, 189.

39. *Idem.*

40. See Marcus P. Ford, *William James' Philosophy: A New Perspective* (Amherst: University of Massachusetts, 1982), chaps. 4, 5.

41. *Process and Reality*, 181, 191.

42. *Ibid.*, 259.

43. "Nietzsche's Prefiguration," 252.

44. "Dispensing with Metaphysics," 55.

45. "Nietzsche's Prefiguration," 243, 247.

46. *Ibid.*, 252.

47. *Ibid.*, 255.

48. *Process and Reality*, 168.

49. *Ibid.*, xiii, xiv, 43, 138-39.

50. *Ibid.*, 129.

51. *Ibid.*, 48, 121.

52. *Ibid.*, 162.

53. *Ibid.*, 143, 162.

54. *Ibid.*, xiii, 11–13.

55. *Ibid.*, 11–12.

56. *Ibid.*, 15.

57. "Nietzsche's Prefiguration," 255 (quoting H. H. Price, *Perception* [London: Methuen, 1964], 3).

58. *Process and Reality*, 122.

59. *Idem.* Whitehead points out, however, that this reference to sensory qualities as "secondary" does not have the consequence in his philosophy that it usually has (*ibid.*, 122). The reason is that (for example) colors as we see them are created by us not out of purely nonqualitative, valueless data (having only the so-called primary qualities), but out of feelings, which are even more obviously qualitative and value-laden than are the secondary qualities into which they are transmuted (*ibid.*, 113–14, 325–26).

60. *Ibid.*, 172.

61. *Ibid.*, 171, 176.

62. *Ibid.*, 129.

63. *Ibid.*, 142.

64. "The Historicist Turn," 48.

65. "Philosophy and the Afro-American Experience," 123.

66. Cornel West, *Prophesy Deliverance! An Afro-American Revolutionary Christianity* (Philadelphia: Westminster Press, 1982), 27, 100.

67. "Nietzsche's Prefiguration," 265; "The Historicist Turn," 40.

68. "The Historicist Turn," 40–42.

69. *Prophesy Deliverance!*, 42.

70. "Frederick Jameson's Marxist Hermeneutics," *Boundary 2* 11 (Fall/Winter 1982–83), 177–200, esp. 195.

71. "Dispensing with Metaphysics," 56.

72. David Bohm, *Wholeness and the Implicate Order* (London: Routledge and Kegan Paul, 1980); Brian Swimme, *The Universe is a Green Dragon* (Sante Fe, N.M.: Bear & Co., 1985); Fritjof Capra, *The Turning Point: Science, Society and the Rising Culture* (New York: Simon & Schuster, 1982); Lewis Thomas, *The Lives of a Cell* (New York: Bantam Books, 1974); James Hillman, *Re-Visioning Psychology* (New York and San Francicso: Harper & Row, 1975); Rupert Sheldrake, *A New*

Science of Life: The Hypothesis of Formative Causation (London: Blond & Briggs, 1981); Charles Birch and John B. Cobb, Jr., *The Liberation of Life: From the Cell to the Community* (Cambridge: Cambridge University Press, 1981); Ken Wilber, *The Atman Project: A Transpersonal View of Human Development* (Wheaton, Ill.: Theosophical Publishing House, 1980), ed., *The Holographic Paradigm and Other Paradoxes* (Boulder, Colo.: Shambhala, 1982), and (with Jack Engler and Daniel P. Brown) *Transformations and Consciousness: Conventional and Contemplative Perspectives on Development* (Boston: Shambhala, 1986); Rollo May, *The Courage to Create* (New York: W. W. Norton and Co., 1955); Robert Bellah et al., *Habits of the Heart* (Berkeley: University of California Press, 1985); Kenneth R. Pelletier, *Mind as Healer, Mind as Slayer* (New York: Dell, 1977); Charles Tart, *Transpersonal Psychologies* (New York: Harper & Row, 1975); Stanley Krippner, *Song of the Siren* (New York: Harper, 1975); Kenneth Ring, *Heading Toward Omega: In Search of the Meaning of the Near-Death Experience* (New York: Morrow, William & Co., 1984); William Irwin Thompson, *Passages About Earth: An Exploration of the New Planetary Culture* (New York: Harper & Row, 1981), and *Pacific Shift* (San Francisco: Sierra Club, 1985); Amory B. Lovins and L. Hunter Lovins, *Brittle Power: Energy Strategy for National Security* (Andover: Brick House, 1982); Charlene Spretnak, *The Spiritual Dimension of Green Politics* (Sante Fe, N.M.: Bear & Co., 1986); Fritjof Capra and Charlene Spretnak, *Green Politics: The Global Promise* (New York: E. P. Dutton, 1984); Carolyn Merchant, *The Death of Nature: Women, Ecology, and the Scientific Revolution* (San Francisco: Harper & Row, 1980); Susan Griffin, *Woman and Nature* (San Francisco: Harper & Row, 1978); Matthew Fox, *Original Blessing: A Primer in Creation Spirituality* (Sante Fe, N.M.: Bear & Co., 1983); Joanna Macy, *Despair and Personal Power in the Nuclear Age* (Philadelphia: New Society Publishers, 1983); Wendell Berry, *The Unsettling of America: Culture & Agriculture* (San Francisco: Sierra Club, 1977); Robert Jay Lifton and Richard Falk, *Indefensible Weapons: The Political and Psychological Case Against Nuclearism* (New York: Basic Books, 1982); Robert Bly, *News of the Universe: Poems of Twofold Consciousness* (San Francisco: Sierra Club, 1980); Willis Harman, *An Incomplete Guide to the Future* (New York: W. W. Norton & Co., 1979); Norman Cousins, *The Healing Heart* (New York: W. W. Norton & Co., 1983) and *The Pathology of Power* (New York: W. W. Norton, 1987); Morris Berman, *The Reenchantment of the World* (Ithaca, N. Y.: Cornell University Press, 1981).

73. Lifton and Falk, *Indefensible Weapons*, 237, 239–43, 255.

8

CORNEL WEST'S POSTMODERN THEOLOGY

William A. Beardslee

The theology of Cornel West responds to postmodern thought and sensibility more directly than does most contemporary theology. His openness to varied strands in what is called postmodern thought affords an opportunity to distinguish fundamentally different types of postmodernism and to ask questions of West as to the deeper affinities of his thought with these differing styles of postmodernism.

The modern, or modernist, period in literature, the arts, and the philosophy related to them, however difficult to define, was characterized by concern for the subject and for a subject that could and did produce visions of the whole. *Modern* has another nuance when we turn to the world perceived as objects, the world of modern science. Here, the struggle was with the seeming determinism of the world of objects and, as we will see, the postmodernism in this science-related strand of culture is characteristically different from that in the humanities. The postmodernism that is found in literary and related philosophical circles is a negative postmodernism, which has turned away both from the subject and from the vision of the whole.

Cornel West welcomes this shift. As someone who speaks for and acts with the Afro-American community, he perceives that visions of the whole are ideological supports for the social powers that have, effectively or ineffectively, organized the political and economic life into a whole. In an article in *Art Papers*, he celebrates the postmodern period because it has been liberating for Afro-American artists. The so-called postmodern period, he says, marks the decisive break-up of the monolithic moral and aesthetic standards that were essentially those of the Western aristocracy or bourgeoisie and opens the way for the expression and recognition of new visions coming from different historical streams.[2]

The same dynamic functions in Professor West's critique of Western philosophy. The great systematic philosophers of the past were unconsciously justifying systems of power. To cite an example in favor of his interpretation: George Pixley, himself a Whiteheadian process thinker, criticized Whitehead for his naive contrast between war and commerce as means of intercourse among nations. Whitehead had spoken of the move from war to commerce as a move from war to peace,[3] but Pixley points out that Whitehead was oblivious to the exploitative, repressive, and colonial structures that made this commerce possible.[4] In a similar vein, West proposes that the deconstruction of philosophical discourse be directed toward uncovering its social function and that the adequacy of a philosophical position be judged in terms of its ability to shed light on and to promote praxis, the transformation of social structures toward the liberation of marginalized persons.

West's postmodernism is thus very different from much of what comes to us under this label. A somewhat sloganized way of putting it would be to say that much of what I am calling negative postmodernism is post-Marxist (insofar as it is poststructuralist), while West's postmodernism is neo-Marxist, being in the tradition of Marxist critical theory. Or we could say that he is a *mediating postmodernist*.

In formal terms, we may say that the more radical or negative postmodernism is postnarrative. Mark C. Taylor, for instance, is critical of Jean-François Lyotard's *The Post-Modern Condition* for the remnants of narrativity in it,[5] and Jacques Derrida's deconstructionist posture is so postnarrative that it leads him to say, in an interview, "I am not a liberationist." Even though he partly takes this back in a later interview, he cannot really be a liberationist because there cannot be a teleology, or connected story, for his activities, as he clearly says.[6]

In contrast to such thinkers as these, it is essential for West's style of postmodernism to retain a narrative vision. Narrative—story that links memory and expectation to the present moment—is the vehicle of hope for the poor, the outsiders, the oppressed. But we should note that a shift occurs in what we may call the locus of narrative. For West, the model of narrative is no longer provided by the story of the moral life of the self as in the great nineteenth-century novels, which have provided the exemplars for most literary analyses of narrative. Rather, his model of narrative is the story of the memories, the hopes, and the liberation of a historical community.[7] If I understand him correctly, West's narrative also differs from the typical story-telling narrative in that it is open, improvisatory, and self-critical, insofar as we are speaking of it in its historical dimension. It does not look forward to a final summation. It is a historical narrativity both in the sense that he turns away from the individual to the story of a community and in the sense that only in the setting of a community to which we somehow belong can we tell a meaningful story. He will not include in his vision of postmodernism that total alienation from community which began to appear in the modernist period and which is a mark of some kinds of postmodernism.

In connection with his awareness of life as lived in community, West rejects the historicism of Richard Rorty, which understands history as the history of ideas, in favor of a "thick historicism," which is able to see ideas and works of art as expressing power relations in society.[8]

One might ask: With so coherent a position, what need does West have for a more explicit philosophical framework, beyond the Marxist theory and (suitably criticized) American pragmatism which express themselves in his work? We have already noted that his is a mediating postmodernism. This means that it is threatened on the one side by reconversion into ideology, a single story, a support for the power of a single element in the social whole (as, indeed, every position is threatened in this way, as West clearly sees), and threatened on the other side by the dissolving forces of the negative form of postmodernism. This form of postmodernism has lost conscious contact with the power to hope for and act in a concerted way for social change and restricts its efforts to negative, deconstructive critique and to the uncovering of spaces for play.

That a position is pressed from different directions is no criticism of it. But perhaps this position could be given added breadth if it were to reconsider the question of the vision of the whole, the rejection of which is so marked a feature of the transition from modernism to negative postmodernism. West is rightly critical of static and ahistorical visions of the whole; he sees their ideological function, and he sees that we are too deeply immersed in our particular histories for a neutral vision of the whole to be a possibility.

Granting these points, the vision of the whole may be more indispensable than the Quine-Goodman-Sellars axis allows.[9] West himself has shown that the affinities between American pragmatism and certain aspects of Nietzsche's thought bring pragmatism perilously close to nihilism, and he cites Nietzsche to the effect that such a development can be avoided only if the breaking of the old forms can be supplemented by "a new world view."[10] In a 1979 article, West dissociates his thought from "philosophy's grand search for invariable, immutable categories in human experience, expression, and language and theology's bold attempt to establish veridical references to a transcendent God." West claims for philosophy the limited tasks of working with theories of historical limits and theories of existential leaps. [11] He has recently expressed more openness to philosophical exploration, but still affirms the strong critique of "old-style metaphysics," especially in our time of "ruins and fragments." [12]

But a vision of the whole is finally necessary for pragmatic purposes. On a pragmatic level, we have to relate our particular histories to others, and our concerns, let us say for the liberation of the poor, to other concerns, let us say for the ecological preservation of the planet. Such a meeting of trajectories calls for the expansion of our horizons and the search for common elements in the various histories and—despite the rejection of this striving by the negative postmodernists—it calls for the quest for directions of convergence in historically separate ventures.

Whiteheadian postmodern thought is a natural ally here because, in the face of the erosion of traditional forms of narrativity, it is able to affirm an intrinsic, open narrativity in experience. [13] Admitting the vision of the whole into West's project allows us to assume that these common elements and convergences are not merely our linguistic and social constructions (which they are, of course, in their expression) but that they may express dynamic elements in the world as well as in our constructions of the world.

The positive vision of Whiteheadian postmodernism is not subject to the criticism that it is making absolutist claims, although it does maintain that, as we move within our local histories to a partial transcendence of them, we can know something about the environment, the history, and even something of the prospects of the context within which we exist. This kind of transcendence of our local histories is very much part of West's concern. I believe that as we enter into movements of partial, and often failing, convergence, fully recognizing the fragmentariness of our actual position, we may see these movements as implying, even requiring, that we are undergirded by a larger whole that is, indeed, itself in process. Furthermore, the Whiteheadian vision of process is an open one, which does not require that complete convergence upon a single end which still appears in many theologies of the future.

The humanistic postmodernism needs to be supplemented by this other type of postmodernism, springing from the new physics and biology and visions of reality such as Whitehead's, for this other postmodernism is much more engaged in the effort to see new forms of integration. [14]

But I would go further. Cornel West, after all, is a theologian. His intellectual tools are able to uncover important aspects of the life of a community of faith. But they are not sensitive to everything that goes on there, nor, by extension, to corresponding aspects of the whole of life that are given concentrated attention in the life of faith. The "transcendent" appears in his vocabulary; but just how does a transcendent reality function in his vision? In some expressions of negative postmodernism, the shattering of structure may momentarily allow us to glimpse that transcendent reality which the structures exclude. [15] This model will fit West's concern for the breaking of oppressive structures. But if we can see that structures may be enabling as well as repressive, then the transcendent may also be revealed in the "daily," even in the midst of the harsh realities of the unredeemed life. The transcendent may even be *active* in daily life. As far as I can see, although a God whose actions can be known in daily life is very much part of West's total picture, his scholarly models do not have space in them for such a God. He appears to resist the kind of vision of continual divine action in the world that is expressed by Whiteheadian theologians, evidently because, in his view, a God who could be expressed in scholarly categories would not be a God to worship. [16]

Whiteheadian theologians believe that West is wrong at this point and that much is to be gained by overcoming the dualism between a scholarship that can speak accurately of the human condition and a faith that speaks of a living God. We need a model of reality and categories with which to order our thoughts that work equally well for our faith and for our scholarly work. I believe that this issue, which is a large one, is at the heart of our dialogue with West. [17]

One concluding note. Whether or not he believes he needs us, it is clear to me that we need Cornel West. As many Whiteheadian theologians have been seeing for some time, our kind of theology needs to be pressed in the direction of the pragmatic engagement and social criticism that lie at the heart of West's work. [18]

NOTES

1. *Art Papers* 10/1 (January–February 1986), 54.

2. West's attention to the importance of aesthetic standards in setting a society's values, and in particular in establishing or criticizing racism, appears also in his analysis of the "classic" standards of beauty formulated by Winckelmann and others; see *Prophesy Deliverance! An Afro-American Revolutionary Christianity* (Philadelphia: Westminster Press, 1982), 53–59.

3. Alfred North Whitehead, *Adventures of Ideas* (New York: Macmillan, 1933), chap. V.

4. George V. Pixley, "Whitehead y Marx sobre la dinámica de la historia," *Dialogos* 7 (1970), 83–107. While recognizing the ideological element in a philosophical system, Pixley nonetheless also recognizes the strength which a criticized Whiteheadian ontology can offer to a philosophy of praxis.

5. In a personal communication from Taylor to the author.

6. See Jean-François Lyotard, *The Post-Modern Condition: A Report on Knowledge*, trans. Geoff Bennington and Brian Massumi (Vol. 10 of "Theory and History of Literature") (Minneapolis: University of Minnesota Press, 1984); for Der-

rida's remarks about liberation, see Robert Cheatham, "Interview: Jacques Derrida," *Art Papers* 10/1 (January–February 1986), 34.

7. See West's "Frederick Jameson's Marxist Hermeneutics," in Jonathan Arag, ed., *Postmodernism, Marxism, and Politics* (Minneapolis: University of Minnesota Press, 1986), 177–200.

8. See Cornel West, "Afterword: The Politics of American Neo-Pragmatism," in John Rajchman and Cornel West, eds., *Post-Analytic Philosophy* (New York: Columbia University Press, 1985), 259–75.

9. For West's pragmatic historicism, see "The Historicist Turn in Philosophy of Religion," in Leroy S. Rouner, ed., *Knowing Religiously* (Vol. 7 of "Boston University Studies in Philosophy and Religion") (Notre Dame, Ind.: University of Notre Dame Press, 1985) 36–51. He writes of his historicism as related to the "mitigated scepticism" of Castellio, Chillingworth, and Pascal (47), and expresses, in what he calls a neo-Gramscian spirit, a preference for local analyses rather than "one grand social theory" (48). At the same time, both here and in his "Frederick Jameson's Marxist Hermeneutics," the central role of narrative vision is clear.

10. See his "Nietzsche's Prefiguration of Postmodern American Philosophy," in Daniel O'Hara, ed., *Nietzsche in Culture* (Bloomington: University of Indiana Press, 1985), 263.

11. "Schleiermacher and the Myth of the Given," *Union Seminary Quarterly Review* 34 (1979), 82.

12. "Dispensing with Metaphysics in Religious Thought," *Religion and Intellectual Life* 3/3 (Spring 1986), 53–56.

13. On Whiteheadian process theology and narrative, see William A. Beardslee, "Narrative Form in the New Testament and Process Theology," *Encounter* 36 (1975), 301–15, and John B. Cobb, Jr., "A Theology of Story," in Richard A. Spencer, ed., *Orientation by Disorientation: Studies in Literary Criticism and Biblical Literary Criticism* (Vol. 35 of "Pittsburgh Theological Monograph Series") (Pittsburgh: Pickwick Press, 1980), 151–64.

14. See Charles Birch and John B. Cobb, Jr., *The Liberation of Life: From the Cell to the Community* (Cambridge: Cambridge University Press, 1981).

15. See John Dominic Crossan, *The Dark Interval: Toward a Theology of Story* (Allen, Texas: Argus Communications, 1975).

16. Although I do not find this point articulated in those of his writings which I have read, West's appreciation of Karl Barth indicates the setting for this judgment.

17. For basic theological statements from a Whiteheadian point of view, see John B. Cobb, Jr., *God and the World* (Philadelphia: Westminster, 1969), and John B. Cobb, Jr. and David Ray Griffin, *Process Theology: An Introductory Exposition* (Philadelphia: Westminster, 1976), especially chap. 3.

18. West himself has noted that, of the various current philosophies of religion, the Whiteheadian form has been the most alert to the need for a political or libera-

tion theology ("The Historicist Turn in Philosophy of Religion," 45). He is referring to Schubert Ogden, *Faith and Freedom: Toward a Theology of Liberation* (Nashville: Abingdon, 1979), and John B. Cobb, Jr., *Process Theology as Political Theology* (Philadelphia: Westminster, 1982).

NOTES ON AUTHORS
AND CENTERS

DAVID RAY GRIFFIN, editor of the SUNY Series in Constructive Postmodern Thought, is author of *God, Power, and Evil, God and Religion in the Postmodern World,* and (with John B. Cobb, Jr.) *Process Theology,* and editor of *The Reenchantment of Science: Postmodern Proposals* and *Spirituality and Society: Postmodern Visions.* He is professor of philosophy of religion at the School of Theology at Claremont and Claremont Graduate School, founding president of the Center for a Postmodern World, and executive director of the Center for Process Studies, 1325 North College, Claremont, California 91711.

WILLIAM A. BEARDSLEE is author of *A House for Hope: A Study in Process and Biblical Thought* and *Literary Criticism of the New Testament,* and editor of *The Poetics of Faith: Essays Offered to Amos N. Wilder.* He is professor emeritus of religion at Emory University and director of the Process and Faith Program of the Center for Process Studies, 1325 North College, Claremont, California 91711.

JOE HOLLAND is author of *Creative Communion: The Spirituality of Work* and (with Peter Henriot) *Social Analysis: Linking Faith with Justice,* and editor (with Anne Barsanti) of *American and Catholic: The New Debate.* He is executive director of PILLAR (Pallottine Institute for Lay Leadership and Apostolate Research), Presidents Hall, Seton Hall University, South Orange, New Jersey 07079.

This series is published under the auspices of the Center for a Postmodern World and the Center for Process Studies.

The Center for a Postmodern World is an independent nonprofit organization in Santa Barbara, California, founded by David Ray Griffin. It promotes the awareness and exploration of the postmodern worldview and encourages reflection about a postmodern world, from postmodern art, spirituality, and education to a postmodern world order, with all this implies for economics, ecology, and security. One of its major projects is to produce a collaborative study that marshals the numerous facts supportive of a postmodern worldview and provides a portrayal of a postmodern world order toward which we can realistically move. It is located at 2060 Alameda Padre Serra, Suite 101, Santa Barbara, California 93103.

The Center for Process Studies is a research organization affiliated with the School of Theology at Claremont and Claremont University Center and Graduate School. It was founded by John B. Cobb, Jr., Director, and David Ray Griffin, Executive Director. It encourages research and reflection upon the process philosophy of Alfred North Whitehead, Charles Hartshorne, and related thinkers, and upon the application and testing of this viewpoint in all areas of thought and practice. This center sponsors conferences, welcomes visiting scholars to use its library, and publishes a scholarly journal, *Process Studies,* and a quarterly *Newsletter.* It is located at 1325 North College, Claremont, California 91711.

Both centers gratefully accept (tax-deductible) contributions to support their work.

INDEX

159